The All-Sufficient Christ

The All-Sufficient Christ

Studies
in Paul's Letter to the Colossians

by

WILLIAM BARCLAY

THE WESTMINSTER PRESS
Philadelphia

LIBRARY OF CONGRESS CATALOG CARD No. 63–18385

PUBLISHED BY THE WESTMINSTER PRESS®
PHILADELPHIA 7, PENNSYLVANIA

PRINTED IN THE UNITED STATES OF AMERICA

Contents

Foreword

I AM VERY GRATEFUL indeed to The Westminster Press for giving me the opportunity and the privilege of writing this study handbook on The Letter of Paul to the Colossians. One thing I should like to say. I have regarded this book as a book written for a distinct and special purpose, and therefore I have not hesitated to say in it things that I have said elsewhere when I thought that it was necessary to repeat them for the sake of the study for which this book was designed. My aim was to write on this letter, as if I had written neither on it nor on the thought of Paul before.

I have, of course, a series of debts to acknowledge. I have made ample use of the great commentaries on Colossians. Those which I have found most useful are as follows. No one can write on Colossians without being indebted to the work of that great New Testament scholar J. B. Lightfoot. I have had always beside me T. K. Abbott's volume on Ephesians and Colossians in the International Critical Commentary. The volume in the older Cambridge Greek Testament by A. Lukyn Williams is a most useful and concise work. The volume in the new Cambridge Greek Testament by C. F. D. Moule bids fair to take its place as one of the best modern commentaries both from the point of view of scholarship and of devotion.

E. F. Scott's volume in the Moffatt Commentary has all his characteristic lucidity and ease. A recent volume, *A New Approach to Colossians,* by L. J. Baggott, makes a valuable contribution to the understanding of the letter.

The older works on the life of Paul by Farr, Conebeare and Howson, and David Smith are still mines of information. I have used C. H. Dodd's older work on the thought of Paul for today, and my own handbook, *The Mind of Paul,* together with the commentary on Colossians in the Daily Study Bible. One of the outstanding new books on Paul is Johannes Munck's *Paul and the Salvation of Mankind.*

All quotations, unless otherwise stated, have been made from the Revised Standard Version of the Bible.

In the transliteration of Greek words the pronunciation is as in English. Only one thing has to be noted. Greek in two cases has two forms of letters that have only one form in English. Greek has two *e* sounds. The one, epsilon, is pronounced as the *e* in the word "yet," and is transliterated simply by the letter *e;* the other, eta, is pronounced either as *ae* or as *ee,* like the *a* sound in "fate" or the *e* sound in "feet," and is transliterated in the form *ē.* Greek has also two *o* sounds. The one, omicron, is pronounced as the *o* in the word "form"; the other, omega, is pronounced as the *o* in "bone." Omicron is transliterated as *o,* omega as *ō.*

It was an ambitious project to choose Colossians as a book for study, for there is no more difficult book in the New Testament. The study of it has opened for myself new understandings of what is one of Paul's greatest letters, and it is my hope and my prayer that this little book may do something to enable others to enter a little more deeply into the thought of this letter.

W. B.

The Letter of Paul

to the

Colossians

(Revised Standard Version)

1 Paul, an apostle of Christ Jesus by the will of God, and Timothy our brother,
2 To the saints and faithful brethren in Christ at Colos'sae:
Grace to you and peace from God our Father.

3 We always thank God, the Father of our Lord Jesus Christ, when we pray for you, 4because we have heard of your faith in Christ Jesus and of the love which you have for all the saints, 5because of the hope laid up for you in heaven. Of this you have heard before in the word of the truth, the gospel 6which has come to you, as indeed in the whole world it is bearing fruit and growing—so among yourselves, from the day you heard and understood the grace of God in truth, 7as you learned it from Ep'aphras our beloved fellow servant. He is a faithful minister of Christ on our[a] behalf 8and has made known to us your love in the Spirit.

9 And so, from the day we heard of it, we have not ceased to pray for you, asking that you may be filled with the knowledge of his will in all spiritual wisdom and understanding, 10to lead a life worthy of the Lord, fully

a Other ancient authorities read *your*.

pleasing to him, bearing fruit in every good work and in-
creasing in the knowledge of God. [11]May you be strengthened with all power, according to his glorious might, for
all endurance and patience with joy, [12]giving thanks to
the Father, who has qualified us[b] to share in the inheritance of the saints in light. [13]He has delivered us from
the dominion of darkness and transferred us to the kingdom of his beloved Son, [14]in whom we have redemption,
the forgiveness of sins.

15 He is the image of the invisible God, the first-born
of all creation; [16]for in him all things were created, in
heaven and on earth, visible and invisible, whether
thrones or dominions or principalities or authorities—all
things were created through him and for him. [17]He is
before all things, and in him all things hold together. [18]He
is the head of the body, the church; he is the beginning,
the first-born from the dead, that in everything he might
be pre-eminent. [19]For in him all the fulness of God was
pleased to dwell, [20]and through him to reconcile to himself all things, whether on earth or in heaven, making
peace by the blood of his cross.

21 And you, who once were estranged and hostile in
mind, doing evil deeds, [22]he has now reconciled in his
body of flesh by his death, in order to present you holy
and blameless and irreproachable before him, [23]provided
that you continue in the faith, stable and steadfast, not
shifting from the hope of the gospel which you heard,
which has been preached to every creature under heaven,
and of which I, Paul, became a minister.

24 Now I rejoice in my sufferings for your sake, and
in my flesh I complete what is lacking in Christ's afflictions for the sake of his body, that is, the church, [25]of
which I became a minister according to the divine office
which was given to me for you, to make the word of God

[b] Other ancient authorities read *you.*

fully known, ²⁶*the mystery hidden for ages and genera-tions*^c *but now made manifest to his saints.* ²⁷To them God chose to make known how great among the Gentiles are the riches of the glory of this mystery, which is Christ in you, the hope of glory. ²⁸Him we proclaim, warning every man and teaching every man in all wisdom, that we may present every man mature in Christ. ²⁹For this I toil, striving with all the energy which he mightily inspires within me.

2 For I want you to know how greatly I strive for you, and for those at La-odice′a, and for all who have not seen my face, ²that their hearts may be encouraged as they are knit together in love, to have all the riches of assured understanding and the knowledge of God's mys-tery, of Christ, ³in whom are hid all the treasures of wis-dom and knowledge. ⁴I say this in order that no one may delude you with beguiling speech. ⁵For though I am ab-sent in body, yet I am with you in spirit, rejoicing to see your good order and the firmness of your faith in Christ.

6 As therefore you received Christ Jesus the Lord, so live in him, ⁷rooted and built up in him and established in the faith, just as you were taught, abounding in thanks-giving.

8 See to it that no one makes a prey of you by philos-ophy and empty deceit, according to human tradition, according to the elemental spirits of the universe, and not according to Christ. ⁹For in him the whole fulness of deity dwells bodily, ¹⁰and you have come to fulness of life in him, who is the head of all rule and authority. ¹¹In him also you were circumcised with a circumcision made without hands, by putting off the body of flesh in the circumcision of Christ; ¹²and you were buried with him in baptism, in which you were also raised with him

---

^c Or *from angels and men.*

through faith in the working of God, who raised him from the dead. [13]*And you, who were dead in trespasses and the uncircumcision of your flesh, God made alive together with him, having forgiven us all our trespasses,* [14]*having canceled the bond which stood against us with its legal demands; this he set aside, nailing it to the cross.* [15]*He disarmed the principalities and powers and made a public example of them, triumphing over them in him.*[d]

16 *Therefore let no one pass judgment on you in questions of food and drink or with regard to a festival or a new moon or a sabbath.* [17]*These are only a shadow of what is to come; but the substance belongs to Christ.* [18]*Let no one disqualify you, insisting on self-abasement and worship of angels, taking his stand on visions, puffed up without reason by his sensuous mind,* [19]*and not holding fast to the Head, from whom the whole body, nourished and knit together through its joints and ligaments, grows with a growth that is from God.*

20 *If with Christ you died to the elemental spirits of the universe, why do you live as if you still belonged to the world? Why do you submit to regulations,* [21]*"Do not handle, Do not taste, Do not touch"* [22](*referring to things which all perish as they are used*), *according to human precepts and doctrines?* [23]*These have indeed an appearance of wisdom in promoting rigor of devotion and self-abasement and severity to the body, but they are of no value in checking the indulgence of the flesh.*[e]

3 *If then you have been raised with Christ, seek the things that are above, where Christ is, seated at the right hand of God.* [2]*Set your minds on things that are above, not on things that are on earth.* [3]*For you have died, and your life is hid with Christ in God.* [4]*When Christ who is our life appears, then you also will appear with him in glory.*

[d] Or *in it* (that is, the cross).
[e] Or *are of no value, serving only to indulge the flesh.*

5 Put to death therefore what is earthly in you: immorality, impurity, passion, evil desire, and covetousness,
which is idolatry. ⁶On account of these the wrath of God
is coming.ᶠ ⁷In these you once walked, when you lived in
them. ⁸But now put them all away: anger, wrath, malice,
slander, and foul talk from your mouth. ⁹Do not lie to one
another, seeing that you have put off the old nature with
its practices ¹⁰and have put on the new nature, which is
being renewed in knowledge after the image of its creator.
¹¹Here there cannot be Greek and Jew, circumcised and
uncircumcised, barbarian, Scyth'ian, slave, free man, but
Christ is all, and in all.

12 Put on then, as God's chosen ones, holy and beloved, compassion, kindness, lowliness, meekness, and
patience, ¹³forbearing one another and, if one has a com-
plaint against another, forgiving each other; as the Lord
has forgiven you, so you also must forgive. ¹⁴And above
all these put on love, which binds everything together in
perfect harmony. ¹⁵And let the peace of Christ rule in
your hearts, to which indeed you were called in the one
body. And be thankful. ¹⁶Let the word of Christ dwell in
you richly, as you teach and admonish one another in all
wisdom, and as you sing psalms and hymns and spiritual
songs with thankfulness in your hearts to God. ¹⁷And
whatever you do, in word or deed, do everything in the
name of the Lord Jesus, giving thanks to God the Father
through him.

18 Wives, be subject to your husbands, as is fitting in
the Lord. ¹⁹Husbands, love your wives, and do not be
harsh with them. ²⁰Children, obey your parents in everything, for this pleases the Lord. ²¹Fathers, do not provoke
your children, lest they become discouraged. ²²Slaves,
obey in everything those who are your earthly masters, not
with eyeservice, as men-pleasers, but in singleness of

ᶠ Other ancient authorities add *upon the sons of disobedience.*

heart, fearing the Lord. ²³*Whatever your task, work heartily, as serving the Lord and not men,* ²⁴*knowing that from the Lord you will receive the inheritance as your reward; you are serving the Lord Christ.* ²⁵*For the wrongdoer will be paid back for the wrong he has done, and there is no partiality.*

4 *Masters, treat your slaves justly and fairly, knowing that you also have a Master in heaven.*

2 *Continue steadfastly in prayer, being watchful in it with thanksgiving;* ³*and pray for us also, that God may open to us a door for the word, to declare the mystery of Christ, on account of which I am in prison,* ⁴*that I may make it clear, as I ought to speak.*

5 *Conduct yourselves wisely toward outsiders, making the most of the time.* ⁶*Let your speech always be gracious, seasoned with salt, so that you may know how you ought to answer every one.*

7 *Tych'icus will tell you all about my affairs; he is a beloved brother and faithful minister and fellow servant in the Lord.* ⁸*I have sent him to you for this very purpose, that you may know how we are and that he may encourage your hearts,* ⁹*and with him Ones'imus, the faithful and beloved brother, who is one of yourselves. They will tell you of everything that has taken place here.*

10 *Aristar'chus my fellow prisoner greets you, and Mark the cousin of Barnabas (concerning whom you have received instructions—if he comes to you, receive him),* ¹¹*and Jesus who is called Justus. These are the only men of the circumcision among my fellow workers for the kingdom of God, and they have been a comfort to me.* ¹²*Ep'aphras, who is one of yourselves, a servant⁹ of Christ Jesus, greets you, always remembering you earnestly in his prayers, that you may stand mature and fully assured in*

⁹ Or slave.

all the will of God. ¹³For I bear him witness that he has worked hard for you and for those in La-odice′a and in Hi-erap′olis. ¹⁴Luke the beloved physician and Demas greet you. ¹⁵Give my greetings to the brethren at La-odice′a, and to Nympha and the church in her house. ¹⁶And when this letter has been read among you, have it read also in the church of the La-odice′ans; and see that you read also the letter from La-odice′a. ¹⁷And say to Archip′pus, "See that you fulfil the ministry which you have received in the Lord."

18 I, Paul, write this greeting with my own hand. Remember my fetters. Grace be with you.

1

The Man Who Wrote the Letter

ALMOST at the same time that a child called Jesus was born in Bethlehem in Judea a child called Saul was born in Tarsus in Asia Minor (Acts 22:3). That child, called Saul, was to become a man who was to do for the Christian faith that which it may be no other man of his generation could have done.

The task of the Christian church was clear and the problem was obvious. Christianity was cradled in Judaism. Jesus was a Jew; all the disciples were Jews; with the single exception of Luke all the New Testament writers were Jews; the ideas and the categories in which the Christians thought were Jewish. And yet inescapably Christianity was a world religion. "Go," said Jesus, "and make disciples of all nations." (Matt. 28:19.) But how was that possibly to be done? The difficulties looked insuperable and the problem looked insoluble.

Amid the world empires Palestine was a tiny country, measuring no more than 150 miles from north to south and 50 miles from east to west. It never had a population of more than four and a half million people. How could anything proceeding from a country like that become a world religion? Worse, the Jews were notoriously hated and despised. Cicero called the Jewish religion "a barbarous superstition" (Cicero, *Pro Flacco* 28), and Tacitus called the Jews "the vilest of people" (Tacitus, *Histories* 5.8). Then as now, anti-Semitism flourished. How could a religion originating among a people hated and despised of all men become a world religion?

Further, the Jews were an exclusive people who despised the Gentiles even more than the Gentiles despised them. They were certain that they were God's chosen people, and equally certain that God had no use for any other people. At their most exclusive they could hold that the Gentiles were made for no other purpose than to be fuel for the fires of hell. They never were characteristically a missionary people. How could Jews possibly come to feel a yearning to bring all other peoples into the love of God?

Into this situation there came a man called Paul. Few men could have come more uniquely from a double background.

Paul was a Jew and Paul was proud of his race. Of his opponents in Corinth he writes: "Are they Hebrews? So am I. . . . Are they descendants of Abraham? So am I" (II Cor. 11:22). To his friends in Philippi he describes himself: "Circumcised on the eighth day, of the people of Israel, of the tribe of Benjamin, a Hebrew born of Hebrews; as to the law a Pharisee" (Phil. 3:5). He had the covenant mark in his body; his lineage was pure; he belonged to the tribe from which the first king had come and he bore that king's name (I Sam. 9:2), the tribe that in the days of the split of the kingdom had been one of the only two that had remained faithful (I Kings 12:21), the tribe that in the battle line of Israel held the post of honor (Judg. 5:12); he spoke the Hebrew language and was not one of those Hellenized Jews to whom the ancient Hebrew was a foreign tongue; he was a Pharisee, one of the Separated Ones, one of the fine flower of Jewish piety.

He so loved his people that he would willingly have

become accursed to save them from their folly of un-
belief (Rom. 9:3). Again and again proudly he says: "I
am a Jew" (Acts 21:39; 22:3; 23:6).

Paul was uncompromisingly a Jew, and proud of the
fact.

Yet this Paul had another background. He was born,
not in Palestine, but in Tarsus in Asia Minor. Tarsus was
indeed no mean city. At the time when Paul was born
into it the university of Tarsus was more famous than
even the university of Athens. Scholars came from the
ends of the earth to study there, and teachers went out
from Tarsus to fill the university chairs in many a city.
There is a thrill of pride in Paul's voice when he describes himself as born in Tarsus (Acts 21:39; 22:3).

Further, Paul was a Roman citizen and born into the
citizenship. Again and again he used that citizenship to
demand the rights of a citizen. At Philippi he brought
the local magistrates to heel with his claim to citizenship
(Acts 16:37–39). In Jerusalem he halted the Roman
tribune in his tracks when the tribune was about to use
the lash on him (ch. 22:24–30). At Caesarea, when he
knew there was no justice for him there, he used his
citizen's right of direct appeal to the emperor (ch.
25:7–12).

Paul grew up in the cosmopolitan atmosphere of
Tarsus, born into the citizenship of Rome. He could not
help thinking in terms of a world.

The problem was how a religion cradled in Judaism
could ever become the religion of the world and of all
men. The answer was Paul, the man designed in the
providence of God to be the bridge between two worlds,
the man who wrote to the Colossians, not with the message of a reformed Judaism, but with the proclamation of
the all-sufficient Christ.

The People to Whom the Letter Was Written

IN PHRYGIA in Asia Minor, in the valley of the River Lycos, there stood a group of three towns. They stood in a glen ten miles long, through which flowed the Lycos on its way to join the Meander, while above them the snowcapped Cadmus range of mountains soared eight thousand feet toward the sky.

Colossae stood at the western end of the glen, and was built astride the river. Eight miles farther up the glen, Hierapolis stood on the northern slopes above the river, and six miles away on the southern side of the river, and in full view of Hierapolis, stood the town of Laodicea. It would have been easily possible to visit all three towns in one day.

Of the three towns, Laodicea was the most important. It was the metropolis of a group of twenty-five towns. It was a great banking center; it was there that Cicero cashed his letters of credit when he was traveling in the district; it was a great road and trading center; and it was one of the wealthiest cities in the ancient world. Hierapolis was famous for its hot medicinal springs; it was a great spa and watering place to which people came from near and far. Colossae itself had once been a great and prosperous town. Xerxes had halted there and Herodotus (7.30) calls it a great city of Phrygia. Cyrus also had

visited it and Xenophon (*Anabasis* 1.2.6) calls it great
and prosperous. But when Strabo came to describe it in
the first century A.D. it was a comparatively small town.
It nevertheless still had its importance because it was on
the main road that led through the Lycos glen on its way
from Ephesus to the Euphrates. It was, however, as
Lightfoot says, the least important town to which Paul
wrote a letter. To this day the ruins of Laodicea and
Hierapolis are clearly identifiable, but even the site of
Colossae is in doubt.

This area had two outstanding characteristics. It was a
volcanic area and it was subject to earthquakes. Strabo,
the geographer, describes it (12.8.6) by the odd adjective *euseistos,* which literally means "good for earthquakes"! It was this feature of the area which gave
Hierapolis its famous hot springs. But the volcanic nature
of the ground had another effect. Volcanic ground is fertile ground, and on the plains of the Lycos valley there
was some of the finest pastureland in the world. And on
them grazed great flocks of sheep, so that the whole area
was famous for its wool and for the garments that were
made from it. Especially around Laodicea there was a
breed of sheep with glossy black wool, from which were
made coats that were famous throughout the world.

The second feature of this area gave it an appearance
that was almost unique in the world. The waters of certain of the streams and rivers in the area are impregnated
with chalk. To this day one of the streams is called Aksu,
which means "the White Water." Pliny tells us that at
Colossae there was a stream into which, if bricks are
thrown, they come out stones (*The Natural History*
31.2). These chalky waters caused the most amazing
growths and incrustations. J. B. Lightfoot describes it:
"Ancient monuments are buried, fertile lands overlaid,
riverbeds choked up and streams diverted, fantastic grot-
toes and cascades and archways of stone formed, by this

strange capricious power, at once destructive and cre-
ative, working silently and relentlessly through long ages.
Fatal to vegetation, these incrustations spread like a white
shroud over the ground. Gleaming like glaciers on the
hillside they attract the eye of the traveler at a distance of
twenty miles, and form a singularly striking feature in
scenery of more than common beauty and impressive-
ness." Herodotus says (7.30) that at Colossae the Lycos
disappeared into an underground chasm and flowed there
for about five stades before it reemerged, and doubtless
the tunnel into which the river disappeared had been
formed by these white chalky incrustations stretching
from bank to bank and thus enclosing the river altogether.

But this too had its use, for, as Strabo tells us
(13.4.14), the nature of the waters made them specially
suitable for use in the dyeing industry, and Colossae was
world-famous for its purple dye, which rivaled even the
dye extracted from the murex shellfish, and which was
made by combining the madder root with these strange
waters.

It can be seen that the three towns were a hive of industry, rich, wealthy, prosperous, and populous.

The people who lived in them fell into three groups.
There were the Phrygians, who were the native inhabitants of the country. There were the Greek colonists, who
had come to live and to trade in these cities. But it so
happened that in these cities there was a third and a very
large group, whose presence without doubt was partly
responsible for the trouble with which Paul had to deal.
There were in Phrygia a very large number of Jews. In
those ancient days it was quite common for kings to
switch whole populations about from place to place; away
back about 200 B.C. Antiochus the Great had taken two
thousand Jewish families from Babylonia and Mesopo-
tamia and had settled them in Lydia and Phrygia. These
Jewish families had prospered, and more and more Jews

joined them, until so many went that the Talmud complained about the Jews who had left their native lands for the luxury of the wines and the baths of Phrygia.

An incident happened in 62 B.C. that shows just how numerous these Jews were. Every Jew, no matter where he lived, had to pay the Temple tax of half a shekel. When a Jew lived outside Palestine this money was remitted to the home country. In that year Flaccus, the governor of Phrygia, was actually alarmed at the amount of currency that was being exported by the Jews in payment of this tax. He ordered that no more money should be sent out of the country. The Jews disobeyed his edict and tried to smuggle the money out to Jerusalem. The money was seized and it amounted to no less than twenty pounds' weight of gold. An amount of gold like that would represent the Temple tax of eleven thousand men; and, since women and children did not pay tax, and since doubtless some money did get out of the country, it would probably not be an exaggeration to say that there were fifty thousand Jews in that part of Phrygia. Beyond a doubt they would have their influence on the community and on the church.

We will conclude this part of our study by looking at Paul's personal connection with the church at Colossae. Paul did not evangelize Colossae personally, nor had he ever been there; he had only heard of how things were going in that church (Col. 1:4). They had never seen his face (ch. 2:1). No doubt the gospel had been preached in Colossae during Paul's long, two-year stay in Ephesus, during which, as The Acts has it, the whole of Asia heard the word of the Lord (Acts 19:10). It is most likely that Epaphras had been the missionary who had been actually responsible for the bringing of the gospel to Colossae (Col. 1:7).

When Paul wrote this letter he was in prison in Rome, awaiting his trial before the emperor. The occasion of

writing may have been twofold. He may have had dis-
turbing news from Epaphras and he may have taken the
opportunity to write when he was in fact sending Ones-
imus back to Colossae to Philemon (Col. 4:9; Philemon
12). The bearer of the letter was Tychicus (Col. 4:7),
who was to supplement the written message of the letter
by word of mouth. So even in prison, with the prospect of
death in front of him, Paul was still thinking of, and
caring for, the churches that were so dear to him. Even
then the "anxiety for all the churches" (II Cor. 11:28)
was on his heart.

3

The Form of the Letter

Few things have shed more light on the New Testament than the discovery of hundreds of letters written by ordinary people to each other in the ancient world. These letters are written on papyrus, and come mainly from Egypt. Papyrus was the writing substance of the ancient world; it was made from the pith of the bulrush cut into strips and then joined and pressed together. So long as it is not subjected to moisture it will last for hundreds of years. So in the ancient world ordinary letters from ordinary people to their friends and their relations were thrown out onto the village rubbish heaps. The sands drifted over the letters and they were preserved just as they were written. In modern times these letters and documents have been systematically searched for and collected. They have then been printed and translated and made available for those who will read them.

Here is one of these letters from a wife who for a time is separated from her husband, whom she loves:

Taus to Apollonius her lord very many greetings. Before everything I salute you, master, and I pray always for your health. I was distressed, my lord, not a little to hear that you had been ill, but thanks be to all the gods that they keep you safe from harm. I beg you, my lord, if it please you, to send for me; else I die because

I do not behold you daily. Would that I were able to
fly and come to you and make obeisance to you; for it
distresses me not to behold you. So be friends with me,
and send for me. Good-by, my Lord. (A. S. Hunt and
C. C. Edgar, *Select Papyri* 1.115.)

Here is another from a lad who had gone to be a soldier
to his father:

Apion to Epimachus his father and lord heartiest greetings. First of all I pray that you are in health and continually prosper and fare well with my sister and her
daughter and my brother. I thank the lord Serapis
(Apion's god) that when I was in danger at sea he
saved me. Straightway when I entered Misenum I received my traveling money from Caesar, three gold
pieces. And I am well. I beg you, therefore, my lord
father, write me a few lines, first regarding your health,
secondly regarding that of my brother and sister, thirdly
that I may kiss your hand, because you have brought
me up well, and on this account I hope to be quickly
promoted, if the gods will. Give my greetings to Capito,
and to my brother and sister, and to Serenilla, and my
friends. I send you a little portrait of myself done by
Euctemon. And my military name is Antonius Max-
imus. I pray for your good health.
    Serenus the son of Agathos Daimon greets you and
Turbo the son of Gallonius. (G. Milligan, *Selections
from the Greek Papyri,* No. 36.)

It can be seen that these two letters—and they are
typical of hundreds—follow the same pattern, and that
pattern is the standard pattern of all ancient letters. They
have, first, a greeting; second, a prayer and thanksgiving;
third, a section containing the special contents of the
letter; fourth, the closing greetings. In addition to these
four sections, many letters have an autographic conclusion, in which the sender, since he could not, or did not,

write the letter for himself, signs his name or makes his mark to guarantee that the letter is his.

The significant thing about this is that this is exactly and precisely the pattern of the Pauline letters. Paul writes his letters in exactly and precisely the way in which ordinary, everyday people wrote ordinary, everyday letters in the ancient world. So in Paul's letters we find the greeting (Rom. 1:1–7; I Cor. 1:1–3; Phil. 1:1–2; Col. 1:1–2); the prayer and the thanksgiving (Rom. 1:8–10; I Cor. 1:4–9; Phil. 1:3–11; Col. 1:3–14); the special contents (Rom. 1:11 to 16:2; I Cor. 1:10 to 16:2; Phil. 1:12 to 4:20; Col. 1:15 to 4:9); the closing greetings (Rom. 16:3–23; I Cor. 16:3–20; Phil. 4:21–23; Col. 4:10–18); and in certain cases the autographic conclusion with the signature of Paul (I Cor. 16:21; Gal. 6:11; Col. 4:18; II Thess. 3:17). The Pauline letters follow exactly the same pattern as the ordinary personal letters of Paul's own day. The pattern may best of all be seen in Philemon, which is so short: first, the greeting (vs. 1–3); second, the thanksgiving (vs. 4–5); third, the prayer (vs. 6–7); fourth, the special contents (vs. 8–22); fifth, the closing greetings and blessing (vs. 23–25).

This fact has certain consequences for our interpretation of Paul's letters. Long ago Deissmann, who was one of the first scholars to use these papyrus letters for the illumination of the New Testament, insisted that the very title "epistle" sets us off on the wrong track in the interpretation of Paul's letters. The epistle is a literary form; from the beginning it is meant for publication; from the beginning it is written with careful and premeditated art. On the other hand, the letter is completely personal; it is written in a definite situation and to meet a definite situation; it is never meant for publication; it is no carefully wrought, literary performance; it is the spontaneous and natural outpouring of the heart of friend to friend.

Deissmann insisted that what Paul wrote was *letters,* and not *epistles.* They were letters, poured out on the spur of the moment, to meet a definite situation, with no conscious literary art, and with no thought that they were going to be collected and published and subjected to the most microscopic examination. "Paul," writes Deissmann, "had no thought of adding a few fresh compositions to the already extant Jewish epistles, still less of enriching the sacred literature of his nation; no, every time he wrote, he had some perfectly definite impulse in the diversified experiences of the young Christian churches. He had no presentiment of the place his words would occupy in universal history; not so much that they would still be in existence in the next generation, far less that one day the people would look on them as Holy Scripture. We now know them as coming down from the centuries with the literary patina and the nimbus of canonicity upon them; should we desire to attain a historical esti-mate of their proper character, we must disregard both. . . . Paul had better work to do than the writing of books, and he did not flatter himself that he could write *Scrip-ture;* he wrote letters, real letters. . . . They differ from the messages of the homely papyrus leaves from Egypt not as letters, but only as the letters of Paul." (A. Deiss-mann, *Bible Studies,* p. 44.) And in another place Deissmann issues the warning: "Almost all the mistakes that have ever been made in the study of St. Paul's life and work have arisen from neglect of the fact that his writings are nonliterary and letterlike in character." (*Light from the Ancient East,* p. 234.)

This warning is very relevant for us in the study that we are about to undertake. We must remember that Paul was not like a theologian, sitting writing in a library, checking every reference, polishing every sentence, weigh-ing every word; he was like a pastor or a missionary, seiz-ing his pen and writing in flaming haste to check some abuse or error before it could spread until it infected the whole body of some church and caused irreparable damage. From this two things will follow.

1. It will not be right to demand from Paul absolute and detailed consistency. He did not read all his letters over before he wrote a new one. It will not be right to insist on following out the logical implications of everything he said to the ultimate and utmost end. Paul was not writing a theological treatise with all the time in the world to do it; he was dealing with a crisis where delay would have been fatal. We must remember that Paul writes in vivid pictures and often in sweeping terms. We must never unduly press a metaphor or insist on following out what seem to us the logical implications of some idea. We must read the letters remembering that they came red-hot from the anvil of Paul's mind, and that often he must have sent them off posthaste without even a second reading of them.

2. It will never be right to demand or expect that Paul will go through the whole of the Christian faith in any one letter. In almost every case he seizes on that part of the faith, that facet of the truth, that particular aspect of Christ and his gospel which the situation demands. That is why Paul's thought is never static, but always in a state of dynamic development. Time and time again he found new visions of Christian truth to meet new situations. It is always true that we discover just as much of Christian truth as life compels us to discover. To take an obvious example, we never really discover and realize and value and appreciate the conception of the life after death until someone who was very dear to us has passed over to the other side. So for each new situation Paul drew new riches from the wealth of Christ. To Paul, Christianity was constantly and consistently a series of

new discoveries, wonder upon wonder, and every one of them true.

We must remember these things, and, when we study Paul's letters, we must study them, not as academic theological documents and epistles, but as living, throbbing, pulsating letters poured out to meet some immediate threat and to help some church that was threatened with the shipwreck of its faith.

4

Trouble at Colossae

To BE ABLE to read only one side of a correspondence is rather like listening in to one side of a telephone conversation. We have the answers, but we do not have the questions that provoked them. We have the advice, but we do not know the situation in which it was given. We do not know the news that Epaphras brought to Paul about the situation in Colossae; and the only way in which we can work our way back to that situation is to try to deduce what it was from what Paul says in the letter itself.

We may begin by noting that the situation in Colossae was as yet a threat more than a disaster. Paul knows and values the faith and the love of the Christians in Colossae (Col. 1:4, 8). There is much in Colossae that was a cause for thanksgiving and not for rebuke.

Paul's methods, when he was confronted with a threatening situation, are a model and a pattern of what our reaction to such a situation should be.

1. Paul believed strongly that prevention is better than cure. He believed in immediate action, so that any threat to the purity of the life and worship and belief of the church might be nipped in the bud before it had time to develop and flourish. He did not believe in waiting and

hoping for the best; he did not believe in evading an issue and a problem in the interests of a spurious peace. He believed that, when evil emerged, it had to be dealt with there and then. He would never allow a situation to develop, because he hesitated to face the problems involved in dealing with it. Many a situation in the church, in the state, and in our personal lives could easily and effectively be dealt with if it was dealt with at once. It is like an illness that is easy to cure in its initial stages, but that may well prove fatal if it is allowed to gain a grip. It is like a fault in a building that can be quickly and cheaply rectified and repaired if it is dealt with at once, but that may well bring the whole building down if action is delayed. It is like a bad habit that can easily enough be eradicated in its early stages, but that, once it gets a grip, becomes an inescapable tyrant over life. We do well to follow the example of Paul, and to act on the principle that prevention is always better than cure. As someone has put it, if on a road there is a sharp bend turning onto a steep cliff, it is better to erect a fence and a danger sign at the bend to prevent accidents than it is to keep an ambulance at the bottom of the cliff to deal with the accident after it has happened.

2. It is typical and characteristic of Paul that it is his almost unvarying practice to begin with praise and congratulation whatever rebuke is to follow. Even in a letter as stern as the First Letter to the Corinthians, Paul begins by thanking God that the Corinthians are enriched in Christ with all speech and knowledge and that they are not lacking in any spiritual gift (I Cor. 1:4–7). Even though the Philippian church has its troublemakers and its mistaken heretics, he begins by telling them that he thanks God every time he remembers them (Phil. 1:3). He will go on to warn and rebuke the Christians of Thessalonica, but he begins by remembering with praise

and gratitude their faith, their love, and their hope
(I Thess. 1:3; II Thess. 1:3). Sternly as he will warn
the Galatians of the peril of the mistaken way that they
are threatening to take, he cannot help remembering that,
when he came to them weak and sick and ill, they would
have plucked out their eyes and would have given them
to him, and that they lovingly received him even though
his condition might well have repelled them (Gal. 4:13–
15). It was with tears of love and sympathy and yearning
that he had admonished the Christians of Ephesus
throughout all his stay among them (Acts 20:31). When
we have cause to rebuke anyone, it is essential that the
rebuke be given in love, and that it appear to be so. Too
often rebuke and warning are given with cold severity,
with conscious superiority, with contemptuous arrogance,
in the spirit that finds a pleasure in seeing someone else
wince, either physically or mentally. There will always
be something good to say, and even in the rare cases in
which there is nothing good to say, there will be something kind to say. It is with such things that Paul so
wisely began—and so must we.

So, then, we now turn to the letter itself to see if we
can deduce from it the nature of the trouble that threatened the life and faith of the church at Colossae. We
shall find our material in two kinds of passages. We shall
find it in passages in which Paul definitely rebukes some
abuse or some error. But we shall also find it in passages
in which Paul specially stresses some facet or aspect of
Christian truth, for the very fact that he does stress such
parts of the truth with passion and intensity shows that
they were either lacking or being transgressed in the
Colossian church. Let us, then, look at both kinds of
passages in the letter.

1. The false teaching was a beguiling seduction (Col.
2:4). It had about it a fascinating and attractive quality

that lured a man to his own destruction. It was like the song of the Sirens, which charmed a man's ears, only to lead him to death and destruction.

2. It was something that could be called philosophy rather than religion (ch. 2:8). It was clever and intellectual, the playground of the mind rather than the refuge of the heart; something that was rather an exercise in mental acrobatics than a way of life to which the whole being could be committed in faith and action.

3. It was based on human tradition (ch. 2:8). In the early church there were certain sects who justified their heretical beliefs and immoral actions on the grounds that there had come down to them a special tradition and revelation apart from that contained in Scripture. They usually actually named some apostle from which that tradition was alleged to have come. They molded life and belief on human tradition rather than on divine revelation.

4. It turned religion into a thing of rules and regulations (ch. 2:20). It identified religion with the observance of certain ritual and conventional acts and practices. It externalized piety. It is still possible for a man to go through all the outward motions of religion with meticulous accuracy and yet to be very far from real Christianity. A man may wear the right clothes, speak the right language, attend the right services, give the right amount of money, allocate the right time to prayer and Bible study, devote the right time to church committees and public service, and yet in his heart there may be pride and self-righteousness and in his life there may be a cold and loveless selfishness and lack of sympathy for his fellow-men and even for those whom he ought above all to cherish.

5. This legalistic spirit issued in certain practices and demands. It issued in laws governing food and drink (ch. 2:16). One of the battle cries of these people was: "Do not handle, Do not taste, Do not touch" (ch. 2:21). Oddly enough, there is hardly any text in Scripture that has been so blatantly misused as this text. It is so often used as a text on which to hang a temperance sermon, as if Paul was instructing people not to handle, not to taste, and not to touch. Paul is, in fact, quoting this as a saying of the heretics and the mistaken teachers, and as an example of the very kind of attitude toward life that a Christian must avoid. It is a warning that Christianity must *not* be identified with the taking of, or the abstaining from, certain kinds of food and drink.

6. It issued in the observance of special days and times and festivals, feast days, new moons, and sabbaths (ch. 2:16). "One man," says Paul, "esteems one day as better than another, while another man esteems all days alike." (Rom. 14:5.) And it is easy to see where Paul's sympathy lies; to him it was only the weaker and more scrupulous brother who made such differentiations. It might be necessary to respect such a man's scruples, but it was not necessary to agree with them. Still less was it necessary to make these scruples the laws of life. The problem still meets us in things like the insistence on making one's Communion at certain times on certain days in a certain way, like the observance of certain people on what they call Sabbath observance. The whole mistake of all such views is that they draw a line between the sacred and the secular, forgetting that there is no such line, for all acts and all days are equally sacred.

Since it is so vexed a question, it will be worthwhile to step aside here for a moment to see certain principles about so-called Sabbath observance.

a. Christians do not observe the Sabbath at all. To talk, for instance, of Sabbath schools is a complete error. The Sabbath is a Jewish institution. Christians observe the Sunday, or, to give it its better name, the Lord's Day.

b. The Sabbath and the Lord's Day are different days. The Sabbath is the last day of the week, our Saturday, and the Lord's Day is the first day of the week.

c. The Sabbath and the Sunday commemorate different events. The Sabbath commemorates God's rest on the last day of the week, and for the Jews its great characteristic was that it was a day of inactivity when all work was forbidden, so that, so to speak, men could reenact God's day of rest. The Lord's Day commemorates the resurrection of Jesus and his rising from the dead, and should therefore be, first and foremost, a day of joy.

d. Jesus said, "The sabbath was made for man, not man for the sabbath." (Mark 2:27.) It will therefore be a first principle that man can do on the Sabbath anything that will be of benefit to his body, mind, and spirit, always remembering that he must demand nothing that will prevent others from also using the day for the benefit of their body, mind, and spirit.

e. It is a fact not without its significance that one of the main causes of the hatred of the Orthodox Jews for Jesus was that they regarded him as a Sabbath breaker and a violater of God's day (Mark 2:23 to 3:6).

f. Even if we do take the Fourth Commandment and transfer it to the Lord's Day—"Remember the sabbath day, to keep it holy" (Ex. 20:8)—we have to remember the basic meaning of the word "holy." Its basic meaning is "different." That which is "holy"—*hagios* in Greek; *kadosh* in Hebrew—is different from other things. The Temple is holy because it is different from other buildings; a priest is holy because he is different from other men; God is supremely holy because he is the Wholly

Other, the One who is different from men. Therefore the
governing principle of the use of the Lord's Day, if this
commandment be transferred to it, is that it should be
different from other days; but that difference will have to
be interpreted in the light of the needs of a man's body,
mind, and spirit.

7. The mistaken notions of the Colossian heretics issued in a rigid asceticism, in rigor of devotion, self-abasement, and severity to the body (Col. 2:23).

Asceticism for its own sake has never been a Christian
obligation or even a Christian virtue. The Jewish rabbis
had a magnificent saying: "A man will give account for
every good thing he might have enjoyed and did not
enjoy." Frank Boreham somewhere tells a story of a man
who in the Rocky Mountains came upon an old Roman
Catholic priest, frail, decrepit, and tottering, but pressing
on. He was so surprised that he asked the old man: "What
are you doing here, father?" "I am seeking the beauty of
the world," said the old priest. "But," said the man
gently, "have you not left it rather late?" Then the old
priest told him his story. All his life he had lived in a
monastery and had hardly set foot outside it. He was very
ill one night, and in the illness he had a vision. An angel
stood beside him. "What have you come for?" asked the
old priest. "To lead you home," said the angel. "Is it a
very beautiful world to which I go?" asked the priest. "It
is a very beautiful world from which you come," said the
angel. "And then," said the old priest, "I remembered that
I had seen nothing of it save the fields and the trees round
the monastery. So I said to the angel: 'But I have seen
very little of the world I am leaving.'" "Then," said the
angel, "I fear you will see very little beauty in the world
to which you are going." "I was in trouble," said the old
man, "and I begged that I might stay for just two more
years. My prayer was granted, and I am spending all my

little hoard of gold, and all the time I have, in exploring the world's loveliness. And I find it very wonderful."

Jesus too explored the world's loveliness. He loved the flowers and the hills and the cornfields and the sea. He loved a feast with his friends. He was no ascetic. There is a wise asceticism in which a person every now and then gives up a pleasure so that he may appreciate it more, and that it may become his joy and not his chain. There is a wise asceticism that avoids all greed and gluttony. But the Christian is a man who remembers always that God gave us all things richly to enjoy.

8. It may well have been that the mistaken teachers of Colossae were also insisting on circumcision. Paul writes that the only circumcision that really matters is not the removal of a certain part of a man's body, but the putting off of his whole lower nature in Christ (Col. 2:11). The important thing is not something physical done to a man's body, but something spiritual which alters a man's whole nature and makes him a new man in Christ.

9. The false worship at Colossae involved the worship of angels (ch. 2:18). Whatever this worship may have been, the angels were being given too high a place within it. This error could have come either from Jewish or from Hellenistic sources.

a. Later Judaism was intensely aware of the transcendence of God, the distance of God from the world, the difference in God, the remoteness of deity from humanity. So great did this distance seem, so unbridgeable was the gulf, that the belief arose that there could be no direct contact between God and the world at all, and that, when God did communicate with the world, he did so by means of intermediaries. We can see this happening even in the narrative of Scripture itself. In the Old Testament story, when Moses went up to Mt. Sinai, God spoke to him face to face, and actually placed the tables of the Ten Commandments in his hands (Ex. 19:19–20; 32:19; Deut. 5:4–5, 22). It was indeed the very fact that God had spoken face to face with Moses and that Moses still lived which provoked the wondering awe of the people (Deut. 5:24). But to the later Judaism, that was an impossible story; it was felt to be quite incredible that God should ever speak directly to any human being; and so the later belief was that the law was given to Moses through the mediation of angels (Acts 7:38; Gal. 3:19). The later Judaism brought angels into the transaction when in the original story there were no angels there.

So in the later Judaism the doctrine of angels was highly developed. Every nation had its angel who held a *prostasia,* a kind of protecting and controlling power over it. Every man had his good and his bad angel. It even came to be said that every blade of grass had its angel.

There is no doubt that there is a certain beauty and loveliness in these ideas, but the fatal thing about them was that they introduced some other being between man and God, so that direct contact between man and God was regarded as impossible.

b. The later Greek thought was just as determined to separate God from the world. The main later Greek idea about God and the gods is that they enjoyed perfect peace and absolute calm and untroubled serenity. The idea was that, if God was involved in the world, he would become worried and anxious and distraught with the care and the burden of it. So the Greeks painted a picture of the gods so completely insulated from the world that they were not even aware of the existence of the world. They do God little honor, said Plutarch, who involve him in the affairs of the world. How, then, was the world governed, controlled, and administered? The world was controlled by the *daimons.* The *daimons* were not *demons.* *Demons* are always bad and evil; *daimons* were the intermediaries between God and man. They controlled the forces of nature, the wind, the rain, and the fire; they brought God's messages to men. They formed a kind of protective barrier between man and God.

Once again the picture is the picture of a world in which direct contact between man and God is an impossibility.

Here is a thought that recurs in all ages of religion. H. G. Wells in one of his novels has a picture of a big-business man, threatened with a complete physical and nervous breakdown. His doctor told him that his only hope was to get hold of something bigger than himself and to hang on to that, to develop within his nervous, tensed, frustrated life fellowship with God. The man answered: "What? Me have fellowship with that up there? I would as soon think of cooling my throat with the Milky Way or of shaking hands with the stars!" To him the very idea of direct contact with the living God was unthinkable.

How different is the confidence of the Christian! The writer to the Hebrews says with joy: "Let us then with confidence draw near to the throne of grace, that we may receive mercy and find grace to help in time of need" (Heb. 4:16). Jesus, he said, has opened for us a "new and living way" into the very innermost presence of God. "Let us draw near with a true heart in full assurance of faith." (Ch. 10:19–22.)

The whole New Testament rejoices in the glorious fact that, once a man knows Jesus Christ, there is nothing between him and God, that the door is wide open for every man. As Paul did, we too must regard with the gravest suspicion any teaching that would put any being between us and God.

10. There is still one other definite charge made against the false teachers in Col. 2:8 and 2:20, but just

what that charge is is far from clear. These two verses present one of the most notoriously difficult problems of translation in the New Testament.

It is interesting to see just what the various translators make of them. The King James Version, the Geneva Bible, the Bishops' Bible and the Revised Version all say that the fault of the teaching of the false teachers is that it is according to "the rudiments of the world," and then go on to say that the Christian in Christ should be dead to "the rudiments of the world." Tyndale and the Great Bible speak about "the ordinances of the world." The Twentieth Century New Testament speaks about "puerile questions of this world." Weymouth speaks about "the world's crude notions," and "the world's rudimentary notions." J. B. Phillips speaks about the false teaching being based on "men's ideas of the nature of the world," and of the Christian being done with "the principles of this world's life." Edgar J. Goodspeed speaks of the false teaching being based on "material ways of looking at things." Ronald Knox speaks about "worldly principles." There is a strong family resemblance among all these translations. But in the Revised Standard Version we come on a completely new idea. It speaks of the false teaching being in accordance with "the elemental spirits of the universe," and says that the Christian should be dead to such spirits. With the translation "elemental spirits" Moffatt agrees; the New English Bible has this translation in the text, but in the margin gives "rudimentary notions." Kingsley Williams speaks of a worldly knowledge "concerned with the forces of nature," to which forces the Christian should be dead. Finally, the Rheims version speaks of "the elements of the world."

It is fairly clear that here there are two main ideas between which the various translations oscillate. One idea is that the false teaching is according to rudimentary and worldly ideas; the other is that it is according to the elemental spirits of the universe. On the face of it, the two ideas are very different. How do they arise, and can we come to any conclusion as to which is to be preferred?

In Greek the phrase is *ta stoicheia tou kosmou. Kosmos* is the world or the universe, and there is neither doubt nor difficulty about it. The difficulty lies in the word *stoicheia. Stoicheion* (the singular form of the word) is a word with a varied and a fascinating history, and if we examine its history, we shall see how the two meanings arise.

a. The basic meaning of *stoicheion* is "anything in a row"; it can, for instance, mean a file of soldiers.

b. It then goes on to mean "a letter of the alphabet," no doubt because the letters of the alphabet are usually set out in rows.

c. It then comes to mean what we call "the A B C of anything," the elementary knowledge of anything; and it is from this meaning that the idea of rudimentary and elementary knowledge comes. The *stoicheia* comprise the elementary knowledge of a subject, beyond which any mature student should long ago have passed.

d. But then the word goes off on another tack. It comes to mean "the elements of which the universe is made."

e. It takes still another and not unconnected step. It comes to mean "the stars" and "the heavenly bodies," and "the signs of the zodiac."

f. And so it comes to take its last meaning; it comes to mean "the spirits who inhabit these heavenly bodies and these signs," or rather, these heavenly bodies and stars regarded as spiritual beings and powers.

With this we come on something that was at the very heart of the life of the ancient world. The ancient world believed implicitly in the power of the stars; the star under which a man was born sealed forever his fate for weal or for woe; there was an iron determinism of the stars. It would not be untrue to say that astrology, as it is called, was the most widespread of all ancient religious faiths. And it is not so very difficult to understand this, for to this day astrology exercises its sway over many a mind, and there are few popular daily newspapers that do not carry a column with information of what the stars foretell for the current day for those born under each sign of the zodiac. There is not a doubt that before a heathen became a Christian he would quite certainly believe implicitly in the power of the stars, the power of the elemental spirits of the universe.

Here, then, we have two perfectly possible lines of thought, both giving a good meaning and both entirely relevant to the situation in the first Christian century. Paul may be saying that these Colossian Christians who should be moving on to maturity in the Christian faith are slipping back into an elementary and superstitious form of religion that they should long ago have left behind. Or he may be saying that these Colossian Christians are still thinking in terms of the power and influence of the spirits of the heavenly bodies and the stars, when they should once and for all have bidden farewell to all such things when they have died and risen to new life with Jesus Christ.

How shall we choose between these two meanings? The word *stoicheia* occurs five other times in the New Testament. It occurs twice in Galatians, in 2:8 and 2:20 and in these passages there is exactly the same doubt as here. It occurs in Heb. 5:12, where there is no doubt that it means a rudimentary and elementary religion that the mature Christian should have long ago left far behind. It occurs in II Peter 3:10, 12, where it without doubt means the elements of the universe which, in the Day of the Lord, will be disintegrated and melted with fervent heat. So the situation really is that the other instances of the word in the New Testament are of little help. The two instances in which the meaning is certain are not relevant; and the one instance in the Galatians passages where the meaning is parallel is also uncertain. On the whole, it is rather more likely that it is the elemental spirits of the universe who are in question, and that Paul is protesting again at teaching that is relapsing into all the superstitious dreads of astrology, for astrology has never failed to exercise a fascination on the minds of men.

Such, then, are the characteristics of the false teaching at Colossae, as far as we can discover them from Paul's actual statements about it. But we have already said that there is another possible line of approach. If there are things that Paul stresses with special force and intensity, we may well assume that they are so stressed because the false teaching denied or ignored them.

1. In this letter we find Paul stressing the inclusiveness of the Christian gospel. He describes his own aim and task: "Him we proclaim, warning *every man,* and teaching *every man* in *all wisdom,* that we may present *every man* mature in Christ" (Col. 1:28). The thrice-repeated "every man" and the phrase "all wisdom" cannot be without significance. "Here," he writes, "there cannot be Greek and Jew, circumcised and uncircumcised, barbarian, Scythian, slave, free man, but Christ is all, and in all." (Ch. 3:11.) It cannot be without significance that the breaking down of the barriers is so comprehensively stressed.

From these passages we cannot be wrong in deducing that there was in the false teaching an exclusive element, that it thought in terms of a spiritual elite, that it drew lines of demarcation instead of obliterating them, that it divided men into classes rather than united them in fellowship, that it was separating and divisive rather than joining and unifying.

2. In this letter we find Paul stressing the all-sufficiency of Jesus Christ more than in any other letter. To the study of this we will return. At the moment we only remind ourselves of the tremendous phrases that Paul uses about Jesus. "He is the image of the invisible God." (Col. 1:15.) "In him all the fulness of God was pleased to dwell." (Ch. 1:19.) In him "are hid all the treasures of wisdom and knowledge" (ch. 2:3). "In him the whole fulness of deity dwells bodily." (Ch. 2:9.) There never was a higher Christology than this. And we can legitimately deduce that the false teaching belittled the all-sufficiency of Jesus Christ, and sought to remove him from the topmost place.

Such, then, was the false teaching at Colossae; and we must now go on to see whether we can succeed in identifying it a little more closely.

5

Threats to the Faith

IN THE BACKGROUND of the New Testament, almost from beginning to end, there lie two threats to the Christian faith. The one was the threat from the world of Jewish thought and belief; the other was the threat from the world of Greek thought and belief. The two threats were not mutually exclusive, and sometimes they came together in one combined threat, as indeed we shall see that they did in the threat that was hanging over the church at Colossae.

1. There was, then, the threat from the Jewish idea of religion, and this threat was twofold.

a. The Jews were always supremely conscious that they were the chosen people, and, if the word "chosen" be rightly interpreted, rightly so. They believed that in God's economy of the world there was a most-favored-nation clause, and that they were that most favored nation. They believed at their most rigid conception that God's interest was confined to them. They could take a text like, "I am my beloved's and my beloved is mine" (S. of Sol. 6:3), and insist that this meant that God belonged to them and they to God to the absolute exclusion of every other nation.

When a Jew who held views like that became a Christian, his belief was that, since Christianity is the greatest privilege and blessing God ever offered and granted to men, it too was for Jews alone. It was the finest flower, the highest peak, the consummation of Judaism. The next conclusion was obvious—anyone who wished to enjoy the benefits of Christianity must first become a Jew. And this belief had one inescapable consequence—to become a Christian a man must first be circumcised, and then become a member of the covenant people.

So these Jews preached circumcision as the necessary precondition of Christianity and the gateway through which a man must enter before he could enjoy the benefits of Jesus Christ. It is to these Jewish Christians that Paul refers when he speaks of the only kind of circumcision that is necessary—the putting off of the old lower nature in the power and the work of Jesus Christ.

The basic and unforgivable fault of these teachers was that they made something done by human hands and by human laws a necessary precondition of salvation. Men were to be saved by the work of men, and not solely by the work of Jesus Christ.

b. The second characteristic of Jewish religion was that it was a religion that was based on works. The rabbis had a saying that a man should think of himself and his fate as being in the balance. Let him do one good work more, and he will win the approval of God; let him do one work less, and he will be condemned. God, they said, deliberately gave the Jewish people the law, so that by obeying its precepts they might acquire more and more merit. This was bad enough when "works" were regarded as deeds of love and kindness and mercy and charity; it was very much worse when "works" were taken to mean obedience to all the ritual laws of cleanness and uncleanness and the like.

However the word "works" be taken, the fact remains that in any such conception of religion a man has to work his passage; he has to earn his salvation; he has to acquire merit; he has to turn a debit balance into a credit balance in the accounting ledger of God. And to the sensitive and sin-conscious soul, that can never be anything other than a losing battle, for creature cannot acquire merit in the eyes of his Creator, nor can the imperfection of man ever satisfy the perfection of God.

The essential fault of such a religion is that it sees salvation as something that a man by merit can win, and not something that in grace God gives. It makes a man think of salvation as something that results from what he is, and not something that results solely from what God is.

Judaism presented a man with a religion, the doorway into which was a rite carried out by the hands of man, and marked only on a man's body, and a religion in which the deciding factor was the merit that a man could acquire by obedience to the law.

To this day there is a certain pride in human nature. There is still a lurking feeling that we can do something to tip the scale of judgment in our own favor. There is still the feeling that we can do something to please God, and worse, that we can do something to put God under an obligation to us, and, as it were, to put God in our debt. A minister, grown old in the service of the church, once told me how he said to a man who was nearing the end of his days: "God has been very good to you," whereat the man replied: "Yes, but I've been not bad to him!"

The very essence of Christianity is that in humble and adoring gratitude we can only accept that which God in Christ so generously offers us.

> Nothing in my hand I bring,
> Simply to thy cross I cling;
> Naked, come to thee for dress,
> Helpless, look to thee for grace;
> Foul, I to the fountain fly;
> Wash me, Savior, or I die.

True, such a love drives us to seek to be worthy of it, but that which we do is not the cause but the consequence of our salvation. Every man is saved *for* works, but no man was ever saved *by* works.

2. But there came from the Greek side of thought that which was in many ways an even bigger threat to the faith. Long before Christianity ever came into the world there had come into life a kind of loathing of the body. Men saw in the body the seat and the moving cause of all sin. *Sōma sēma,* said the Orphic catchword, "the body is a tomb." Plato could speak of the prison house of the body. "I am a poor soul shackled to a corpse," said Epictetus. Seneca could speak of "the detestable habitation of the body." This line of thought could and did end in the most far-reaching consequences.

The ancient thinkers asked the question that all men have asked in every age: Whence comes evil? Whence comes sin? In answer to this question there came into life a type of thought called by the general name of Gnosticism. Gnosticism was founded on a thoroughgoing dualism. Its beliefs may be summarized as follows. In the beginning there were two entities, spirit and matter. There never was a time when there was no matter; matter is as eternal as God. Spirit is God, and spirit is altogether good. Matter from the first, even before time began, had an essential flaw in it. It is out of this flawed matter that the world is made; the stuff of the world is bad stuff; and hence comes all the evil of this world.

Since matter is evil, the true and only real God who is spirit could not touch and handle that matter himself. And yet out of that matter the world had to be made. So the true and real God put out a series of aeons or emanations from himself. Each aeon was farther from the true God than the one that went before. Further, each successive aeon became more and more ignorant of the true

God, as the aeons became more distant from the true
God. As the distance from God of the series of aeons in-
creased, not only did the aeons become more and more
ignorant of God, they became also more and more hostile
to God. At last at the end of the chain there was reached
an aeon so distant from the true and real God, who is
pure spirit, that it could touch and handle matter; and it
was by that aeon that the world was created. That is to
say, the world was created by a power utterly ignorant of,
and completely hostile to, the true and real God. We are
living in a world made out of bad stuff, made by a
power distant from, ignorant of, hostile to, the true and
real God. That—and no wonder—is why the world
is evil. Hence come sin and suffering and sorrow and
evil. It is not that something mendable has gone wrong
with the universe; it is that the universe is essentially and incurably and irremediably evil. Clearly,
this belief has far-reaching consequences for life and
belief.

a. It had the most serious effects on Christology.

(1) It obviously makes it impossible to believe in
the incarnation in any real sense of the term. If matter
is evil, then the body is evil, and therefore into the body
God could never have come. The Gnostic theory was
worked out on the basis that it is impossible for God to
have any contact with matter. So there arose what is almost the first of all the great Christological heresies, the
heresy of Docetism. The word "Docetism" comes from the
Greek verb which means "to seem," and literally means
"seemism." It held that Jesus never had a real body, that
he only appeared to have a body, that his body was nothing more than a kind of phantom apparition. Jerome
wrote, "While the apostles were still surviving, while
Christ's blood was still fresh in Judea, the Lord's body
was asserted to be but a phantasm." Even in New Testament times this heresy was there, for John in his letters

identifies with Antichrist those who denied that Jesus
Christ had come in the flesh (I John 4:1–3; II John 7).
In the apocryphal Acts of John it is said that Jesus left
no footprint on the ground when he walked, and that
when he was touched there was no body there to feel
(Acts of John 93). Marcion, as Tertullian said, held that
Jesus had only a *corpus phantisticum,* "a phantasmal,
ghostly body."

It is easy to see that this would have an attraction for
a world that in any event believed the body to be essentially evil. Augustine said that in the writings of the
philosophers of Greece he could parallel practically every
statement in the New Testament except one: "The Word
became flesh" (John 1:14).

(2) Sometimes these Gnostics allowed a kind of limited incarnation. They held that the spiritual Christ
descended into the man Jesus and left him again before
he was crucified. No Gnostic could ever believe that the
true and real God was involved in suffering and pain and
agony. Cerinthus held that it was Simon of Cyrene who
was crucified, while the real Christ looked on and
laughed. In the Acts of John (97) there is an extraor-
dinary passage in which the real Christ is described as
talking to John on the Mount of Olives at the very time
that the man Jesus is being crucified on Calvary. "John,
unto the multitude below in Jerusalem I am being crucified and pierced with lances and reeds, and gall and
vinegar is being given me to drink. But to you I am speaking and listen to what I am saying." In the apocryphal
Gospel of Peter the cry of dereliction on the cross becomes: "My power, my power, you have forsaken me"
(4:19), and is the cry of the man Jesus when the
spiritual Christ has withdrawn from him. So Gnosticism
presents us with the picture of a Christ who could never
know what suffering is.

Apart altogether from suffering, the Gnostics held that

the spiritual Christ did not and could not undergo any human experience that is part of manhood. Marcion held that the Christ appeared in Palestine a man full-grown, because he could not undergo the processes of birth. Many Gnostics did hold that Jesus was born in a kind of way, but that he simply passed through Mary like, in a strange simile, water through a pipe. Even an orthodox Christian like Clement of Alexandria held that Jesus had none of the feelings, passions, impulses, emotions that are part of manhood.

Those who truly loved Jesus Christ and those who passionately believed in the incarnation saw the terrible danger of this kind of belief which, with a kind of mistaken reverence, destroyed the real humanity of Jesus. Ignatius speaks scathingly of those who said of Jesus that "his suffering was only a semblance." Passionately he says of Jesus that he was truly born, that he truly ate and drank, that he truly suffered, that he was truly persecuted, that he was truly crucified, that he truly died, and truly rose again (Ignatius, *To the Trallians* 9, 10). What is left of the gospel if the body of Jesus was no more than a ghostly phantom and if his sufferings were no more than a ghostly shadow play without reality?

(3) It will be best if we go through the whole perversion of Christianity by Gnosticism before we look at Paul's resounding answer to it. The next mistake in which Gnosticism issued was a denial of the uniqueness and the full divinity of Jesus Christ. The Gnostics had drawn their picture of the long series and ladder of emanations between man and God. They then went on to say that Jesus was no more than a link in that chain; he might even be the highest link; but he was no more than one of these many beings who were intermediaries between God and man. To them he was no longer unique; he was simply one of many, even if he was the highest of many. The direct and unique unity of Jesus with God was gone, and

at the best Jesus ranked only with the highest of the prophets.

b. This false, Gnostic teaching had the most serious consequences on the ethical conduct of its followers. Gnosticism begins from the conviction that matter is evil. If matter is evil, then the body is evil. Nor is the body evil in the sense that it is sinful and needs to be cured and reformed. It is *essentially* evil, and nothing that can ever be done to it can possibly make it anything else. This issued in two quite logical, but nevertheless diametrically opposed, attitudes toward the body.

(1) It issued in a rigid asceticism. If the body is evil, then all its wishes and desires must be denied, all its appetites must be refused their satisfaction, its needs must be cut down to the irreducible minimum, it must be punished and buffeted, as you would scourge and buffet an enemy. So in the third and fourth centuries we come to the great age of the ascetics. They starved themselves until they became lean, gaunt, and emaciated. To take a bath or to care for the body became a sinful thing, and they became so neglected and filthy that "lice dropped from them as they walked," which was looked on as a sign of special holiness. "Why," demands Jerome, "should Paula add fuel to a sleeping fire by taking a bath?" The more beautiful the body was, the more dangerous it was. Jerome insists that a child's nurse should never be fresh and young and lovely, but always old and misshapen and ugly. There came the age of the pillar saints of whom the most famous was Simeon Stylites. These pillar saints lived in little cages on the top of pillars which each year they raised a little higher from the ground. Many of them spent years in this self-chosen isolation, never coming down. There came the age of the *inclusi,* the shut-up ones. These *inclusi* had themselves bricked up in a little niche in the wall, with nothing but a slit left for air to

enter and for the bare minimum of food to be slipped in
to them.

Asceticism and contempt of the body became a badge
of honor in the church. We may well either laugh or
stand appalled at such excesses; but at the same time we
may well ask, Has the Christian church ever really got
over its suspicion of the body? Is it not the case that to
this day there is a lurking feeling that sex is something
unclean? Is the so common failure in sex education a survival of this fear of the body? We do well to remember
that the contempt and fear and hatred of the body spring
from a heresy and not from the true faith. And we do
well to remember that Paul said that the body is the
"temple of the Holy Spirit" (I Cor. 6:19), and that he
pled with men to present these same bodies as a living
sacrifice to God (Rom 12:1).

(2) But this Gnostic attitude toward the body could
and did issue in the exact opposite of this asceticism. It
could and did issue in the most sensual and sordid immorality. This attitude could be arrived at in three different ways.

First, it is the nature of the body to be evil. Therefore,
when the body is used for lust and immorality it is simply
fulfilling its own nature, and to fulfill its own nature is a
good thing.

Second, if the body is evil, then it does not matter
what it does. Nothing can make it better and nothing can
make it worse. Therefore, let it glut and sate its appetites.
It makes no difference what is done with and to the
body, for the body is in any event an evil thing.

Third, there was the most dangerous line of all. It was
claimed that the true Gnostic was so secure in his own
illumination and his own special knowledge that he could
allow himself the most sensual and gross sins and excesses,
and take no harm from them. What mattered was his soul,
his spirit. It was secure in its perfectly illuminated fellow-

ship with God; nothing that the body could do could taint and infect it.

The false teaching of Gnosticism wrecked the Christian ethic whichever line it took. It could turn ethics into a fanatical asceticism, in which the body was regarded as an incurably evil thing; or it could turn ethics into an orgy of immorality on the ground that physical things, being evil, are of no importance.

c. Finally, this Gnosticism has the most disastrous effect on the fellowship of the church. If matter is evil, then the supreme aim of life must be the escape of the soul from the body, the release of spirit from matter. The soul, in order to reach God, had to climb up the long ladder of aeons which stretched between man and God; somehow or other it had to get past each of the aeons in the series between this material world of evil and the spiritual realm of good. In order to do that it needed all kinds of special passwords and all kinds of special knowledge. It was, in fact, the right knowledge that alone could liberate a man from matter and enable him to reach spirit.

Well and good—but the next step is the fatal step. It was held that such knowledge was available for only a select few. The great majority of mankind were quite incapable of attaining to it. They were such that they had not the ability to learn this liberating knowledge, and they must be content to remain forever within the material world, while their superior brethren climbed through the spheres to fellowship with God. The inevitable result was the creation within such circles of a religious aristocracy, a spiritual elite, who looked down on their lesser and earthy brethren. The fellowship of the church was shattered, for it was divided into those for whom real religion was possible and those for whom it was not.

It was in the face of this that Paul insisted that there was possible full, mature Christianity for *every* man (Col.

1:28), and that in Christianity the differences were wiped out and obliterated forever (ch. 3:11).

Here, then, was the threat to the faith of the Christians at Colossae. From the Jewish side they were threatened with the danger of a faith that was conditioned by that which human hands could do and that which human goodness could attain. On the Greek side it was threatened by a teaching that wrecked the incarnation, that destroyed the Christian ethic, and that rendered impossible the fellowship that should exist within the Christian church.

What made the situation in Colossae doubly serious was that the two threats had combined into one. When we have examined the false teaching in Colossae, and when we have seen it in the light of these two threats, we must then see that it has elements from both of them. It had, for instance, an element that stressed human laws and regulations, which is Judaism; and it had an element that belittled the place of Christ and destroyed Christian fellowship, which is Gnosticism. But in the ancient world it not infrequently happened that renegade Jews and Greek Gnostics joined forces in a kind of unholy alliance. We have already seen that the Gnostics insisted that special knowledge and special preparation were needed to climb and to rise past the long ladder and series of aeons between man and God. It was here that the Jews came in and claimed that it was precisely their law with all its rules and regulations that gave and provided that special knowledge. And so the speculations of Gnosticism and the legalism of Judaism joined in a threat to the Christian faith.

Colossae may have been the least important town to which Paul ever wrote a letter, but he wrote it in answer to a threat so perilous that it might well have wrecked the Christian faith.

6

The All-Sufficient Christ

WE HAVE SEEN the peril that threatened the church at Colossae. We have examined the false teaching, and we have identified it, and we have seen what its consequences would have been for faith and life if it had been allowed to flourish, to develop, and to spread unchecked. And now we turn to look at Paul's answer to it. Paul did not take the negative method of arguing with and contradicting the false teachers; he took the method of stating the Christian gospel in all its splendor. The false teachers had tried to remove Jesus Christ from the topmost niche and had tried to despoil him of his uniqueness. Let us see Paul's answer. We begin by setting down the main passages in which Paul's counterblast is contained.

He is the image of the invisible God, the first-born of all creation; for in him all things were created, in heaven and on earth, visible and invisible, whether thrones or dominions or principalities or authorities—all things were created through him and for him. He is before all things, and in him all things hold together. (Col. 1:15–17.)

Christ, in whom are hid all the treasures of wisdom and knowledge. (Ch. 2:2–3.)

For in him the whole fulness of deity dwells bodily, . . . who is the head of all rule and authority. (Ch. 2:9–10.)

We have here Jesus Christ in a series of relationships.

1. There is Jesus *in his relationship to God.*

a. Jesus is "the first-born of all creation." It may well be that here we have a phrase which in its English dress is misleading. The word for "firstborn" is *prōtotokos,* and it has two connected but quite distinct meanings.

First, it has what may be called a *time* meaning, and it does mean quite simply born first in point of time. So, for instance, Adam is said to be the firstborn man. If that meaning is taken here, it will simply mean that Christ was the first of created persons to be born; it will quite definitely look upon him as a part of creation; it will involve him in creation rather than separate him from creation. Now, the whole tenor of Paul's thought forbids us to take that meaning, for Paul is concerned to show, not that Jesus is simply a part of creation, but that he is above and beyond creation; and in any event Paul goes on to say that all things were created by him and that he was before all things. This means that we must seek the meaning of *prōtotokos* along its other line.

Second, *prōtotokos* came to indicate *primacy* far more than *priority.* The process by which it developed this meaning is by no means difficult to follow. The firstborn son is the son who has the special place of prestige and honor. He is the father's heir and successor; he has a unique place in the family that cannot be shared by any other son. So the word *prōtotokos* comes to have the atmosphere far more of primacy in honor rather than mere priority in time.

"Israel," says God, "is my first-born son." (Ex. 4:22.) Israel was certainly not the firstborn nation in point of time, but Israel was certainly the firstborn nation in the plan and the design and the heart of God. God says of the Davidic king:

And I will make him the first-born,
the highest of the kings of the earth.
(Ps. 89:27.)

There quite clearly the word "first-born" has to do with place and prestige and honor and not with time at all. Jacob, who became Israel and who gave his name to the nation, is called God's firstborn; there again it must mean that Jacob stood high in the honor of God. And, most significant of all, in the rabbinic writings God himself is called the firstborn of creation, which can only mean that God is the sovereign of all creation.

So when Jesus Christ is called the firstborn of all creation, it does not mean that he was the first created person to be born; what it does mean is that to him God has assigned the first place, the lordship, the sovereignty of all creation. Here, therefore, the translation of the New English Bible is much to be preferred: "His is the primacy over all created things." First, then, Paul lays down the sovereignty of Jesus Christ over the whole creation of God.

b. Before that, Paul has already called Jesus "the image of the invisible God." The word is *eikōn*. This word is a regular word for that which is a precise copy, reproduction, or replica. Gregory of Nazianzus defines an *eikōn* as a replica of an archetype. It is used, for instance, of the head of a king on a coin, or of the statue of a famous man. It is used in Heb. 10:1 of that which is real in opposition to that which is merely shadowy and imperfect.

But this word *eikōn* has two very significant uses. Insofar as there is any word in Greek for any such thing— which of course in the ancient days did not exist—it is the word for a "photograph." Apion, the soldier, writes home to Epimachus, his father, in the letter that we have already quoted: "I send you a little portrait of myself done by Euctemon." The word for "portrait" is *eikōnion*, which is the diminutive form of *eikōn*. And, further, *eikōn* has a still more suggestive use. There were certain business transactions, such as the issuing and acknowledging of an I.O.U. or a receipt for money paid, in which the identification of the person or persons involved was of the first importance. To these documents was attached an accurate, detailed, easily recognizable description of the person involved, and that description is called an *eikōn*. An *eikōn* is an accurate picture or description of the person involved.

So, then, to call Jesus the *eikōn* of God is to say that Jesus is the perfect portrait of God. If you wish to see what God is like, look at Jesus; in Jesus the invisible God becomes visible to men. So, then, as Lightfoot puts it, this word *eikōn* says of Jesus, first, that he is the perfect *representation* of God. But ordinarily we can go and look at the person of whom the portrait or the description is a representation. We cannot do that in the case of the infinite and the invisible God; so not only is Jesus the *representation* of God; he is also *the perfect manifestation and revelation of God*. In one sentence, in Jesus we see God. When we look at Jesus, we can say, This is what God is like. And what a blinding revelation to see God in the one who healed the sick, and fed the hungry, and comforted the sorrowing, and chose ordinary men to be his right-hand men, and was the friend of those whom the conventional and the orthodox and the pious regarded with contempt and supercilious disgust. Here indeed is a revelation that changes a man's whole relationship to God.

2. Next there is Jesus *in his relationship to the world*. We have already seen that he has the primacy over all created things. But there is much more than that. In him and through him all things were created. All things hold

together in him. All things were created for him. He is the *agent* of creation; he is the *sustainer* of creation; he is the *goal* of creation. He is, as the John of The Revelation has it, "the Alpha and the Omega, . . . the beginning and the end" (Rev. 22:13). Let us look at this.

a. Jesus Christ is *the agent of creation.* The aim and design of this statement is obvious. The Gnostics, the false teachers, drew their picture of a world created by a god who was a totally inferior god, a god ignorant of the true God and hostile to the true God. The Gnostics drew their picture of an evil world created out of evil matter by an evil god. No! says Paul resoundingly. The world was not created by an evil god like that; it was created by the one who is the true image of the true God. Now this has certain far-reaching implications.

First, we are back here in the first chapter of Genesis with that refrain that runs through the whole Creation story like the ever-recurring motif in a symphony—and God saw that it was good (Gen. 1:4, 10, 12, 18, 21, 25, 31). Certainly this world is not what it was meant to be, but fundamentally it is good, because it is the handiwork of one who is the very expression of God. Earth is not a desert drear. Thomas Hardy tells of Tess thinking of the universe in her simple way. She thinks, not of one world, but of a whole host of worlds. She thinks of them like apples on the stubbard tree—some of them fair and good, others blighted. "Which kind do we live on?" she was asked. And her answer was: "A blighted one." That is precisely what the world is not. That is the Gnostic view of the world, but not the Christian view. The world "means intensely and it means good."

b. If we believe that Jesus Christ is the agent of creation, then we must believe that *the principle on which the world has been created is the principle of love.* If Jesus Christ is the agent of creation, then we must believe that the principle of creation is the same as the principle of redemption. There will come times in life when this conviction will be the one thing in the world left to hang on to. When completely inexplicable things happen to us, when things happen that torture the body or wound the heart or bewilder the mind, it will make an infinite difference if we can be sure that somehow or other the power behind all this is the power of love.

Hardy finished his story about the tortured life of Tess with the sentence, "The President of the Immortals had finished his sport with Tess." If we have nothing left to believe except that at the heart of things there is a cynical power that makes a mockery of men, then life becomes intolerable. But if we can believe that, however much life hurts, at the heart of it there is love, then even the sorest thing becomes bearable. For then we can share the faith of which Browning wrote in *Paracelsus:*

> God! Thou art love! I build my faith on that.
>
> . . . .
>
> I know thee, who hast kept my path, and made
> Light for me in the darkness, tempering sorrow
> So that it reached me like a solemn joy;
> It were too strange that I should doubt thy love.

The connection of Jesus Christ with creation is not simply a cosmological dogma or speculation. It is an affirmation of faith that the love which was operative in redemption is the same love which is operative in creation, and that, therefore, the principle of the universe is love.

c. As Paul sees it, Jesus Christ is not only the agent of creation, he is also the one in whom "all things hold together" (Col. 1:17). It would be perfectly possible to think of a creator who made the world and then left the world to itself, of one who, as it were, set the world going and then left the world to its own devices. A watchmaker, for instance, may make a watch, but once he has made it and sold it, it is out of his hands. But to Paul, Jesus Christ was more than the creating power and personality; he is, as J. B. Lightfoot puts it, "the principle of cohesion in the universe." He makes the universe "a cosmos instead of a chaos," an ordered and orderly and reliable whole instead of an erratic and unpredictable muddle. This is a very great thought.

As the early thinkers saw it, Jesus Christ is the principle of cohesion in the *physical universe*. This is not a thought that is familiar to us, but it was perfectly familiar to the early Christian thinkers. This is exactly the thought in the conception of Jesus as the Logos, the Word. The first person to strike upon this conception of the Logos lived in Ephesus six hundred years before Jesus came to the world; his name was Heraclitus. Heraclitus saw two principles in the world complementing each other. He began by saying, "Everything is in a state of flux." Everything is continuously changing and nothing remains the same. "You cannot," he used to say, "step into the same river twice." Step into it; step out of it, step into it again, and you have stepped into a different river. And yet in spite of this state of flux there is a reliability and dependability in nature and in the world. The same reaction always follows the same action; the spring, summer, autumn, and winter come back in unvarying order; every species begets its own species; and the universe is such that you can make deductions and calculations knowing that they are correct. There must then be another principle in the universe besides the principle of flux. What is that other principle? It is the Logos. "All things happen according to the Logos." And the Logos is the Divine Reason, the Divine Mind, interpenetrating the universe, making it a cosmos and not a chaos.

The Christian said, "Jesus *is* that mind of God." He who created the universe put his own laws into the universe. As Lightfoot put it, "The law of gravity is an *expression* of his mind." There is something very great here. The laws of nature are the laws of God. It is because the mind of God, the Logos, the Divine Reason, the Son, Jesus Christ—they all mean the same—is in and through the universe that the universe has the marvelous order and the dependable, reliable, predictable order that it has. The scientist, the mathematician, the astronomer, the nuclear physicist, if they only knew and realized it, are discovering the laws of God all the time, and it is his reason that guides them. The universe is as it is, because the Spirit of Christ is in it to order and to control.

There is something that we can see much more easily than that. *Jesus Christ is the principle of cohesion in society.* Unless society is Christian society, it is disintegrated society. The feature of life without Christ is that it is essentially divided; class is divided against class, color against color, ideology against ideology. Politics, for instance, cannot produce a united society. H. M. Hyndman, the labor agitator, when he was an old man said, "I used to think that social democracy would take the place of religion, but now I see that human beings want something more."

In the ancient world, the church was literally the only place in the world where all men of all classes and conditions could and did meet in perfect fellowship together. They *cohered* in Christ. In the early church, master and slave sat together in a *cohesion* they could not find anywhere else in the world. James Black drew a dramatic, imaginary but true, picture of the kind of thing that could happen in the early church. A great man, a VIP, is touched for Christ. He comes to his first service. The Christian leader meets him. "Will you come and sit here?" he says. The great man says: "But that man is my slave. I can't sit beside him!" Quietly the leader repeats, "Will you please sit there?" "But—" says the man. Gently but insistently the leader again repeats, "Will you please sit there?" And suddenly light floods the face of the man;

he walks across and sits down; he gives his slave the kiss of peace. Master and slave are one in Christ—praise God!

In Christ all kinds of men and women *cohere.* The church is the one place in the world where there are neither class nor color distinctions. If such distinctions do exist in a so-called church, it is not a church. It is merely a human group of men and women who have not even begun to discover what Christianity means.

Still further, *Jesus Christ is the principle of cohesion among nations.* There were times when men clearly saw this. In the fourth century, Rome was still a great empire; but, to those who had ears to hear, the whole structure was creaking. Out on the frontiers the barbarians were pressing in; at the center there was a rot of the moral fiber that was terrifying. It was then that Constantine decided that Christianity must be the religion of the Empire, and as John Foster tells in *Then and Now,* it was then that Constantine said that he was handing the Empire over to the church "to set in order the body of the world, laboring under grievous sickness." Christianity was the one thing in which a mad universe could cohere.

We shall not save the universe with armies or with atomic weapons; the split atom can but mean the split world; only in Christ can the nations, disintegrated in hatred, cohere in love. What a responsibility is laid on the Christian today! Will we take it? John Foster in the book just quoted tells of one of the great missed chances in history. In 1271 the greatest empire in the world—the greatest empire the world has ever seen—was the empire of the Mongol Kublai Khan. It stretched from the Ural mountains to the Himalayas, and from the China Sea to the Danube. Kublai Khan in that year sent Nicolo and Maffeo Polo as his ambassadors to the pope with a request.

You shall go to your high priest and shall pray him on our behalf to send me a hundred men skilled in your religion

. . . and so I shall be baptized, and when I shall be baptized
all my barons and great men will be baptized, and then their
subjects will receive baptism, and so there will be more
Christians here than there are in your parts.

The East was wide open to Christ. But the pope was too
busy playing politics. For eighteen long years precisely
nothing was done, and not a man was sent. Then in 1289
a mere handful of missionaries were dispatched—too late
and too few—and the chance was gone. Think of it. If
the church had seized the chance, there would have been
no such thing as Mohammedan Turkey, no such thing as
pagan India, no such thing as Red China. The East
would have been Christian from end to end. What a
vision! What a tragedy! What a different world it might
have been today!

Today again there is a heaven-sent chance for the
Christian to witness to the fact that he believes—and he
proposes to act on the belief—that *only in Christ* can the
world cohere.

So, then, in the physical universe, in society, and in
the nations Christ alone is the principle of cohesion.

d. But we are not finished with the relationship of
Christ to the world. *Christ is the goal and the end of all
creation.* "All things were created through him *and for
him.*" (Col. 1:16.) The world was created to be nothing
less than, and nothing other than, the Kingdom of Christ.
Tremendous flights of thought open up here. Suppose
we think in terms of evolution and the evolutionary
process. It is then possible to think of Jesus Christ as the
peak and the crown of the evolutionary process. Man in
Jesus Christ at last reached his destiny, for in Jesus Christ
we see man as the image of God, which he was meant to
be (Gen. 1:26). A. J. Gossip, great saint and scholar,
my own old teacher, had an adventurous mind and could
say the most startling things. Sometimes he would say that
the dream of God is a world of Christs, a world where

every man has reached the stature of Christ, the perfect man. That is another way of saying that Christ is the end of the universe, its goal, its purpose, and its aim. What a challenge is here! As G. K. Chesterton said, "Whatever else is true of man, it is certainly true that man is not what he was meant to be." Life was never meant to be the dreary, weary, frustrated thing it is. Life was meant to be Christ. The world exists for Christ; men were created to be his and to be like him.

3. Next there is Jesus *in his relation to the unseen world.* "In him all things were created, in heaven and on earth, visible and invisible, whether thrones or dominions or principalities or authorities—all things were created through him and for him." (Col. 1:16.) Thrones or dominions or principalities or authorities—strange words. These are, in fact, the names of grades and classes of angels and spirits who lived in the various heavens, from the seventh heaven downward.

As we have already seen, the ancient world believed implicitly in angels, spirits, and demons. And all these angelic and spiritual and demonic powers were out to work men harm. The ancient world was a terrified world. It was said that you could not so much as lift the point of a needle in the air but it came against one of these unseen powers of whom the air and atmosphere were full. "The air," as Samuel Dill says in *Roman Society from Nero to Marcus Aurelius,* "was tremulous with superstitious fear." "Life was the sport of inscrutable powers of the unseen universe." The ancient world believed in "gods in every grove and fountain, and on every mountain summit; gods breathing in the wind and flashing in the lightning, or the ray of the sun and the star, heaving in the earthquake or in the November storm in the Aegean." The ancient world was demon-haunted, so that men were afraid to look over their shoulder. Even the philosophic Gnostics, with their aeons, erected a legion of spiritual forces intent on stopping man from reaching God.

Paul too believed in these demonic powers, for he was a man of his age. But he has something to say. Jesus Christ created these powers, and on his cross he disarmed them, and made a public example of them, and dragged them behind him in beaten submission like a general dragging his captives in a Roman triumph (Col. 2:15). It is as if he said to the Colossians: "You need not fear even the demonic powers of the invisible world, for Christ made them, and Christ mastered them, and Christ broke their power forever."

Missionaries tell us that one of the greatest reliefs that come to heathen peoples is the sudden realization that they do not have to fear and cope with hundreds of malignant gods and spirits, but that there is only the one God whose name is love.

Maybe this all seems very remote to us, who are emancipated from the belief in demons and the like. But sometimes there comes to every one of us the feeling that we are living in a hostile world, that there is a demonic power in things which is out to break us. Lessing said that, if he had one question to ask the Sphinx, that question would be: "Is this a friendly universe?" Dick Sheppard tells of the night, when in the dark he felt what he could only call the spirit of the universe, and when he was filled with the desire to shout out: "Friend or foe?"

The Christian knows that there is no force or power or being, seen or unseen, in all the universe, who is greater than Christ. With Christ he is safe, for Christ is the Victor Christ, and in Christ there is nothing that can "separate us from the love of God" (Rom. 8:35–39).

4. There is, finally, in the passages that we are studying *the relationship of Jesus to all other self-styled and alleged revelations of God.* "In him all the fulness of God

was pleased to dwell." (Col. 1:19.) In him "are hid all the treasures of wisdom and knowledge" (ch. 2:3). "In him the whole fulness of deity dwells bodily." (Ch. 2:9.) In these statements of Paul there are three counterblasts against the propaganda of the false teachers.

a. Paul lays it down that *Jesus needs no supplement.* In him are *all* the treasures of wisdom and knowledge. The Gnostic position was that the so-called simple message of the gospel was well enough for simple and unlettered and unspiritual Christians, but that they possessed a still further and a still fuller revelation. Paul states quite bluntly that there can be no fuller revelation than Jesus Christ.

There is a danger that threatens always to imperil the Christian faith. It is the danger that comes from syncretism. Syncretism is that attitude toward religion which holds that no one religion can be said to possess or to offer the whole truth, and that the way to a world religion is to take the best from all religions and to mold it all into a new religion that is an amalgam of all existing religions. The idea is that the message of Christ has to be filled out by material from other sources. On this point Paul is uncompromising. There is no one who can add anything to Jesus Christ. In Jesus Christ there came to men the full and final and perfect revelation of God, and we need nothing more.

b. Paul lays it down that *Jesus brooks no rival.* To the Gnostic false teachers, as we have seen, Jesus was simply one of the many intermediaries between God and man. He might be the nearest to God; he might be the highest of all; but he was certainly not unique. The word Paul uses for "fulness" is *plērōma.* This was itself a Gnostic word; the Gnostics used it to describe the absolute complete perfection of the true God. It was exactly that, says Paul, that dwelt in Jesus Christ. In Jesus Christ we do not see a part of God; we do not have a partial revelation;

in Jesus Christ we see the whole of God in relation to
men; and that revelation is given to us in no one else,
for Jesus Christ is unique.

c. Paul lays it down that *this complete revelation is
made* in incarnation. He is the fullness of deity *bodily*.
Both in the English and in the Greek the word "bodily"
(*sōmatikōs*) comes at the end of the sentence, and comes
like a hammerblow. Here is Paul's insistence once again
that the revelation of God did not come in one who was
a ghostly and immaterial phantom but in one who was
as truly man as he was truly God, and who was as truly
human as he was divine.

So, then, Paul presents us with a picture of what Jesus
Christ is in relation to the world, in relation to God, in
relation to the unseen powers, in relation to all other
revelations so called; and in every case he finds him all-
sufficient and unique.

7

The Work of Christ

O F ONE THING the whole New Testament is completely sure—that all that Jesus Christ did in his
life and in his death was for us men and for our salvation.
When Paul wrote the letter to the Colossians he was not
writing a treatise on the atonement; nevertheless, there
is in this letter a remarkably full picture of the work of
Jesus Christ. In it there is a series of great pictures of
what Jesus did.

Before we look at these pictures, we would do well to
note one fact which for Paul was the basis of everything.
That one fact is that behind the whole work of Christ
stands God. There is a way of presenting the work of
Christ as if it actually consisted in pacifying God, in
making God withhold his hand when it was poised to
strike. There is a way of speaking about the atonement
in which Jesus Christ and God are almost set over against
each other, a presentation that leaves us with the picture
of a gentle and loving Jesus whose one desire was that
men might be forgiven and a stern and hard God whose
one desire was that men might be justly punished for their
misdeeds and their disobedience. There is never anything
like that in the thought of Paul. For Paul the whole
scheme of redemption began in the heart of God; the
action in redemption is the action of God; it is God who

sent Christ, and God who is in Christ; the basis of everything is the love of God and the great desire of the heart of God that all men should be saved (I Tim. 2:4). Let us then look at the great pictures that Paul uses in this letter to describe the work of Christ and the action of God.

1. Paul thinks of the atonement in terms of *God's deliverance of man.* "He [God] has delivered us from the dominion of darkness and transferred us to the kingdom of his beloved Son." (Col. 1:13.) Here even more vividly the New English Bible speaks of "the domain of darkness."

There is here a picture of a practice that was not uncommon in the ancient world. Sometimes in the ancient world, after a victorious campaign in which a country was subdued and subjected, the conqueror would transfer the whole population of that country to some other place and bring a new population in. The most famous example of that was, of course, the taking away of the ten tribes of Israel to the land across the Euphrates after the conquest of the Northern Kingdom, an exile from which they never returned and in which they became the lost ten tribes. So, then, in the ancient world it was literally possible for a people to be transferred from one domain to another.

Of course, the transference from one kingdom to another was not always so dramatic as that. It was perfectly possible for a people to find themselves part of some new kingdom, under some new king, and included in some new empire. Now what must be understood is that there were times when this was an event for which a people might give sincere and hearty thanks. That was particularly the case in the greatest days of the Roman Empire. There were actual cases when kings on their death willed their kingdoms to Rome. Especially in the East there were peoples who for years and centuries had been under the rule of bloodthirsty and unpredictable Eastern tyrants, in circumstances in which justice did not exist, and no man's life and property were safe from capricious rulers. The provincial, as Edgar J. Goodspeed points out in his *Introduction to the New Testament,* was often profoundly grateful for the change. "The provincial, under Roman sway, found himself in a position to conduct his business, provide for his family, send his letters, and make his journeys in security, thanks to the strong hand of Rome." For him it was a privilege to be transferred from one kingdom to another.

So Paul says that God delivered us from the domain of darkness and brought us into the Kingdom of his Son. Such a deliverance is the widest and the most comprehensive deliverance possible. But we can distinguish at least three things in it. (*a*) Through Jesus Christ we are delivered from the darkness of ignorance and brought into the light of knowledge. In him we gain the knowledge of God and of goodness; in him we learn what to believe and what to do. (*b*) Through Jesus Christ we are delivered from the darkness of sin and brought into the light of holiness. Through Jesus Christ the tyrannous power of sin is broken and a new goodness becomes possible, for, as James Denney always insisted, whatever else is true, it is always true that Jesus Christ makes bad men good. (*c*) We are, here again, at the thought that so constantly recurs in this letter. The powers of darkness were the demonic powers which, in those days men believed, haunted the universe. The sway of these demonic powers is broken forever, for on his cross and in his resurrection Jesus Christ disarmed and despoiled them (Col. 2:15). In Jesus Christ we are transferred from a demon-haunted to a Christ-filled universe.

2. Paul thinks of the work of Christ in terms of *reconciliation to God.* In Christ it was God's aim to reconcile all things to himself (ch. 1:20). Men who were

once estranged from God, and whose minds were hostile
to God, are reconciled to him (ch. 1:21–22). Paul describes this as "making peace." For the Jew the meaning
of the word "peace" was "right relationships"; and this
means that through the life and the death of Jesus we
are enabled to come into a right relationship with God.

This has always been the simplest and the most human
way of expressing what Jesus has done for us. To put it
at its simplest, through him it has become possible for
us to become friends of God. The most ancient tragedy
and the most universal tragedy in life is the breach of
personal relationships, the situation in which two people
drift apart until there stretches between them a gulf of
misunderstanding, across which it is very difficult to build
a bridge. There is a famous papyrus letter called the letter
of a prodigal son. It is from a son to a mother whose heart
he has broken. Here is part of it:

Antonis Longus to Nikous his mother many greetings. Continually I pray for your health. Supplication on your behalf
I direct each day to the lord Serapis. I wish you to know that
I had no hope that you would come up to the metropolis.
On this account neither did I enter the city. But I was
ashamed to come to Karanis because I am going about in
rags. I write you that I am naked. I beseech you, mother, be
reconciled to me. But I know what I have brought upon myself. Punished I have been in every way. I know that I have
sinned. (G. Milligan, *Selections from the Greek Papyri*, No.
37.)

In Greek there exists a collection of model letters for every
occasion compiled by a writer called Proclus (*De forma
epistolari*); and one of the strangest commentaries on
human nature is that in it (the twelfth letter), there is a
letter that is a model for all prodigals to use:

I know that I have erred in that I have treated you ill. Therefore, having repented, I beg pardon for the error. But for

the Lord's sake, delay not to forgive me. For it is just to pardon friends who stumble, and especially when they desire to obtain pardon.

The prodigal is a permanent character in the human drama. "I beseech you, mother," wrote Antonis Longus, "be reconciled to me." And the word he used is closely kin to the word Paul uses for our reconciliation to God (*dialassein* and *apokatalassein*). It is as if God said to men in Christ, "Be friends with me again." It is not God who has ever to be reconciled to men; the door of his heart was and is forever open. It is man who has to be reconciled to God, in the stubbornness and the pride and the rebellion of his heart. In Jesus Christ, God pleads with men, and in Jesus Christ, God opens the way back to himself for every prodigal son.

3. Paul sees the work of Christ in terms of *redemption*. This is an idea that is common in the New Testament. "The Son of man . . . came . . . to give his life as a ransom for many." (Mark 10:45.) "You were ransomed from the futile ways inherited from your fathers, not with perishable things such as silver or gold, but with the precious blood of Christ, like that of a lamb without blemish or spot." (I Peter 1:18–19.) So Paul speaks of the Son, "in whom we have redemption" (Col. 1:14). To put it at its simplest, redemption is liberation at a cost. It so happens that this was an idea that would be real and meaningful and vivid to both Jews and Greeks.

The greatest event in the whole history of Israel was God's redemption of his people when they were slaves in Egypt. This was the event that was stamped and imprinted on the memory of the nation; this was the event that had brought them into a special and unique relationship with God, for in it God had acted for them as he had acted for no other people. This was the event that they were forbidden ever to forget. "You shall remember that you were a slave in the land of Egypt, and the Lord your God redeemed you." (Deut. 15:15; 24:18.) Israel knew what redemption was like.

But this conception was equally real and vivid to the Greeks. In his book *The Atonement in the Light of History and the Modern Spirit,* David Smith points out that in New Testament times the payment of a ransom price was something for which every traveler, or the relatives and friends of every traveler, had to be prepared. It was the age of pirates and of brigands. On land and at sea a man might well be captured and held for ransom, until the price of his liberation was paid. After the Battle of Adrianople in the fourth century, Ambrose, the great Bishop of Milan, spent all he had to ransom the captives, and, when that was not enough, he melted down the sacramental vessels themselves and coined the metal into money; and when he was charged with sacrilege, he replied that the souls for which the Lord's blood had been shed were more precious than the vessels that contained that blood. As David Smith points out, one of the features of the liturgies of that age is that again and again they remember the captives and the prisoners. Even in the New Testament itself the writer to the Hebrews says: "Remember those who are in prison" (Heb. 13:3). Clement of Rome prays: "Save our afflicted; pity the lowly; raise the fallen; manifest thyself to the needy; heal the ungodly; restore the wanderers of thy people; ransom our captives." In the Liturgy of St. Mark there is a prayer for "them that are holden in prisons or in mines or in exile or in bitter bondage, pity them all, deliver them all." In the Liturgy of St. James there is this petition: "Remember, O Lord, Christians at sea, on the road, among strangers, those in mines and tortures and bitter bondage, being our fathers and brethren." During the war when there were many of our friends and dear ones in prison camps and worse than prison camps these prayers became suddenly relevant again. In ordinary times they have little relevance because, even if there are still notorious kidnapping cases, for the most part this kind of thing does not arise.

The meaning is that men were in bondage to the power of sin, and it cost the life and death of Jesus Christ to set them free. Because of their sin and because of the sin of the whole world, men were in a state of estrangement from God, like prisoners in a camp far from home, and the only thing that could set them free and bring them home to God was that which Jesus Christ did for all mankind.

4. Paul thought of the work of Jesus Christ in terms of *forgiveness*. He speaks of the Son "in whom we have redemption, the forgiveness of sins" (Col. 1:14). He speaks of God canceling the bond that was against us and nailing it to the cross (ch. 2:14). There are two vivid pictures here.

a. The word for "forgiveness" is *aphesis*. In the Old Testament this word has one special meaning and one special connection. It refers regularly to remission of debts and letting go free which, according to the law, were to happen in the seventh year and in the year of jubilee. Every Hebrew slave was to serve for six years, and in the seventh year he was to go out free. At the end of every seven years every creditor was to release what he had lent to his neighbor and was not to exact it (Ex. 21:2–11; Lev. 25:39–46; Deut. 15:1–18). This remission and liberation are called *aphesis*. That is to say, *aphesis* is the cancellation of an obligation; it is the releasing of a man from a debt and an obligation that might have been held over him and extracted from him. So, then, through Jesus Christ we are released from the unpayable debt under which we were to God. As Wesley had it: "No condemnation now I dread."

b. The word *aphesis* was just as meaningful to a Greek audience as it was to a Jewish one. It was the regular word for the remission of taxes or for exemption from taxation. So in Egypt, certain land, especially land used for sacred purposes, was *en aphesei,* in a state when taxes were canceled and remitted. Once again we have the same idea; *aphesis* is the cancellation of a debt that might have been exacted, the remission of an obligation that a man would have been forced to discharge, the release from a debt that a man could have been compelled to pay.

Every living man is immeasurably and unpayably in debt to God, and through the work of Jesus Christ that debt is remitted and forgiven.

c. We get the same idea repeated in an even more vivid picture in another part of the letter. "God . . . having canceled the bond which stood against us with its legal demands; this he set aside, nailing it to the cross." (Col. 2:13–14.) The bond is a *cheriographon,* literally a "note of hand." It is the Greek for an I.O.U., a bond entered into which states and acknowledges a debt, and makes payment of it obligatory, and sets out certain penalties if payment is not duly and completely made. It was an obligation like that under which we were to God; and that bond which stood accusingly against us is canceled and annulled.

There are two further parts of the picture, for one of which there is abundant and certain evidence, and for the other of which there is a suggestion that may or may not be true.

First, there were two Greek words that Paul might equally well have used to express this idea of cancellation. Both had a vivid picture in them; either would have served his purposes, and it may well be not without significance that he chose the word he did choose.

We take first the word Paul might have chosen, but

did not choose. The Greek word for canceling a document is often *chiazesthai,* which means to mark with the letter *chi,* which is shaped like a capital X and pronounced like the *ch* in the Scottish pronunciation of *loch.* A large cross was drawn across the pages of a canceled document. Clearly that would have given Paul a vivid picture, for it would have meant that the charge against us was canceled forever, because it was marked with the cross. And yet Paul did not use that word.

We now take the word that Paul did use. It is the word *exaleiphein,* which means "to sponge or to wipe off." Ancient ink was very black, and it lasted for a very long time; but in it there was no acid; it therefore did not at all bite into the paper. It did not need to be erased, to be rubbed or scraped off; it could be sponged off; and so part of a scribe's equipment was a sponge with which he simply wiped off the paper that which he wished to delete or correct. This is the word that Paul uses. The bond that stood against us is sponged away, wiped off.

There is this difference in the pictures of the two words. When the bond or charge against a man was canceled with a *chi,* crossed out, the charge was still there, and beneath the cancellation it was still plainly and perfectly readable; it was canceled, but it was not obliterated. On the other hand, when the charge or the bond was wiped off with the sponge, it was as if it had never been; it was canceled *and* obliterated.

It is perhaps not reading too much into this passage to think that Paul deliberately chose this word. God does not only forgive our sins; he even obliterates the memory of them. We all know that there are two kinds of forgiveness. There is the kind of forgiveness that forgives but that certainly does not forget. A man may forgive in the sense that he does not exact the penalty and the punishment that he had the right to exact, but forever afterward he, as it were, holds the old mistake over the head of the

person who made it. Often he reminds him of it, and
sometimes with a kind of unconscious blackmail he uses
it as a lever to compel the "forgiven" person to do as he
wishes. There can be a certain kind of forgiveness that
remits the penalty but is very far from true reconciliation.
On the other hand, there can be a forgiveness that forgives
and forgets.

Someone tells how once a book by Andrew Lang was
savagely and viciously and quite unjustly reviewed by a
young and arrogant journalist. Andrew Lang was hurt
by the sheer injustice of the review. Some years later that
same young journalist wrote a book. Andrew Lang was
found reading the young man's book and obviously enjoying it. Someone said to him: "Surely you cannot be
reading the book that impudent young cub wrote." And
then to his complete astonishment the friend found that
Andrew Lang had no memory at all of the attack made
upon himself. He had not only forgiven, he had completely forgotten. A forgiveness like that, the friend felt,
was almost divine.

The forgiveness of God is such that God not only
cancels our penalty and our punishment and the charge
against us, he obliterates it. He does not ever hold
it against us; he treats us in his amazing love as if it had
never been.

Second, Paul says that this record of our sins was nailed
to the cross. There are two possibilities here. It is sometimes said that in the ancient world, when a decree became obsolete and when it was no longer operative and
when it was canceled, it was fixed to a public notice board
and a nail was driven through it to show that it no longer
had any force. If this is the meaning, the picture is that
the record of our debts and misdeeds is fixed with a nail
to the cross to show that it no longer has any force and
no longer stands against us. But scholars are doubtful if
there ever was any such custom, although quite possibly

there may have been. The other picture will be that the
accusing record is crucified itself; the accusing record itself stands condemned; its life and its reign and its demand are ended, and by the cross of Christ we are freed
forever from the debt of our sins. For the sake of Jesus
Christ the guilty have become the innocent in the eyes
of God.

5. Paul thought of the work of Jesus Christ in terms
of *the bringing of hope*. He speaks of "the hope laid up
for you in heaven" (Col. 1:5). He speaks of "Christ in
you, the hope of glory" (v. 27). If there was one thing
more than another that Jesus Christ brought to men, it
was hope; and he brought hope in a double sense.

a. He brought *hope for this world*. One of the strange
and tragic features of the age to which Christianity first
came was its defeated hopelessness. It was not that that
age did not know its sin; it did know it, but it had come to
the conclusion that there was nothing that anyone could
do about it. Persius, the Roman poet, prays to the gods to
punish tyrants "that they may look on virtue and pine that
they have lost her forever." Seneca, the Stoic moralist,
comes back again and again to a kind of doctrine of the
total depravity of man. "We are wicked, have been, will
be. Every age complains of the decline of morals. The
form of vice may change, but it remains the same." "We
have all done wrong, and shall go on doing it to the end
of the chapter." What Seneca longed for above all was
"a hand let down to lift us up." But that there was such
a hand, or, if there was, that that hand should be
stretched down to us, he had no hope.

Into that defeated, pessimistic, hopeless, frustrated
world there came Christianity. It was not so much that
Christianity brought new moral teaching; there is, in fact,
very little in the Christian ethic that cannot be paralleled
in pagan ethics; but what Christianity did bring was a

moral dynamic. Paul writes to the Christians in Corinth, and Corinth was maybe the worst city in the ancient world from the point of view of morals: "Do you not know that the unrighteous will not inherit the kingdom of God? Do not be deceived; neither the immoral, nor idolators, nor adulterers, nor homosexuals, nor thieves, nor the greedy, nor drunkards, nor revilers, nor robbers will inherit the kingdom of God." (I Cor. 6:9–10.) What a list! What a picture of society lies behind it! But Paul does not stop there. Suddenly on the heels of that catalog of crime there comes the triumphant shout of victory: *"And such were some of you"* (v. 11). Christianity brought to men and women who were morally defeated, and for whom goodness and purity were only haunting and un-attainable visions, a hope to light the darkness of their despair, and a dynamic to make them what they knew they should be and had never been.

b. He brought *hope for the world to come*. It took men a long time to come to any certainty that death was not the end. It took Jesus Christ and his work to "deliver all those who through fear of death were subject to life-long bondage" (Heb. 2:15). Neither world to which Christianity went out had any real hope of a life to come.

(1) The Jews in Old Testament times had no real hope of a life beyond the grave. As they thought of it, all men alike, when they died, went to Sheol. Sheol is not hell; Sheol was a gray, shadowy land in which the dead lived a pale, colorless, strengthless, joyless existence, like ghosts and shades and shadows, separated alike from God and from man. True, there was some kind of existence, but it was the existence of a shadow rather than a person. Again and again we meet this gray pessimism in the pages of the Old Testament. "In death there is no remembrance of thee; in Sheol who can give thee praise?" (Ps. 6:5.) "Whatever your hand finds to do, do it with your might;

for there is no work or thought or knowledge or wisdom in Sheol, to which you are going." (Eccl. 9:10.) "Sheol cannot thank thee, death cannot praise thee; those who go down to the pit cannot hope for thy faithfulness." (Isa. 38:18.) "There is hope for a tree, if it be cut down, that it will sprout again, and that its shoots will not cease. . . . But man dies, and is laid low; man breathes his last, and where is he? . . . So man lies down and rises not again; till the heavens are no more he will not awake, or be roused out of his sleep." (Job 14:7, 10, 12.) True, every now and again there are glimpses to lighten the darkness. "I know that my Vindicator lives, and at last he will stand upon the earth; and after my skin has been thus destroyed, then without my flesh I shall see God." (Job 19:25–26.) "Thou dost guide me with thy counsel, and afterward thou wilt receive me to glory." (Ps. 73:24.) But these are only fitful flashes in the dark. For the Jew, the world to come offered nothing better than existence as a shade.

(2) The Greek thought about the life to come, and even yearned for the life to come, but he could never be sure. It is true that in the *Phaedo,* Plato laid on the altar of hope the greatest of all merely human pleas for a life to come, but it is maybe not too much to say that no one was really convinced. In Homer, Achilles tells Odysseus that he would sooner be a hired laborer, alive on earth, working for a man of no substance, than the king of all the dead. In the *Anthology,* Ptolemy speaks of himself as "a mortal and the creature of a day." "The later paganism," as T. R. Glover grimly put it, "believed in death." At the best all that the great pagans could say was *if* and *perhaps.* Tacitus ends his noble tribute to the dead Agricola: "If there be any habitation for the spirits of just men, if, as the sages will have it, great souls perish not with the body, mayest thou rest in peace." *If.* Cicero speaks of the thoughts of men about life after death and

then says wistfully: "Which of these opinions is true, some God may know." Euripides writes agnostically in the *Hippolytus* (Gilbert Murray's translation):

> But if any far-off state there be
> Dearer than life to mortality,
> The hand of the Dark hath hold thereof,
> And mist is under the mist above;
> So we are sick for life, and cling
> On earth to this nameless and shining thing,
> For other life is a fountain sealed,
> And the deeps below are unrevealed,
>   And we drift on legends for ever.

To the Stoics, God was a fire, purer and clearer than any earthly fire. That which gave men life was that a spark of that divine fire came and dwelt in a man's body; and when a man died, the spark returned to be reabsorbed in the fire which is God. No kind of personal existence there. Epicurus, strangely enough, made it his lifework to destroy the belief in immortality. He believed that that belief was the cause of nothing but fear, and he wished to banish it forever. To that end he produced his atomic theory. In the beginning there was nothing but space, and atoms falling through space in long straight lines like rain. But the atoms were given power to swerve. When they swerved they bumped into each other, and so formed oscillating masses. And everything in this world, you and I and everyone and everything else, is nothing other than, and nothing more than, a fortuitous conglomeration of atoms. So is the soul, and all that happens in death is that the soul disintegrates, just as the body does, and the atoms fly free. Atoms thou art and to atoms thou shalt return.

These were the dreams of the poets and the speculations of the philosophers. But to the ordinary man there was no hope, and so death was a parting forever and ever.

There is extant a papyrus letter written by a woman called Irene to sympathize with—one cannot say to comfort— her friend Taonnophris on the death of a child:

Irene to Taonnophris and Philo, good cheer! I was as much grieved and wept over the blessed one, as I wept for Didymas, and everything that was fitting I did and all who were with me, Epaphroditus, and Thermouthion, and Philion, and Apollonius and Plantas. But truly there is nothing that anyone can do in face of such things. Do you therefore comfort one another. Good-by. (G. Milligan, *Selections from the Greek Papyri,* No. 38.)

There tender sympathy and hopelessness combine to produce a pathos that has in it all the tears of things. "I was not; I became; I am not," says the bleak inscription on the pagan tomb. Catullus pleads with his Lesbia to give him a thousand kisses and yet another thousand, for, when life's brief day is done, there remains nothing but one long night through which man must forever and forever sleep a sleep that knows no awakening.

Into that world of death came the ringing message of the Christian hope, the message that, because Jesus Christ lives, the Christian shall live also (John 14:19), the message that nothing in life or in death, in time or in eternity can separate the Christian from the love of God in Christ Jesus his Lord (Rom. 8:38–39). There comes the triumphant shout of Paul: " 'Death is swallowed up in victory.' 'O death, where is thy victory? O death, where is thy sting?' . . . Thanks be to God, who gives us the victory through our Lord Jesus Christ" (I Cor. 15:54– 55, 57).

Through the work of Jesus, death forever lost its terror.

6. Paul thought of the work of Jesus Christ in terms of *the bringing of life.* The Christian has "come to fulness of life in him" (Col. 2:10). Christ is our life (ch. 3:4).

Without Jesus Christ a man may exist, but he cannot
live. The Romans told how once there came to Julius
Caesar a weary, lackluster, dispirited creature with the
request to be permitted to commit suicide and to stop
living. Caesar looked pityingly at him. "Man," he said,
"were you ever alive?" In Christ, life attains a vividness,
an intensity, a thrill, a vitality, which without him it
could never have achieved. Even in so short a letter as the
letter to the Colossians, Paul has much to say about this
life.

a. It is the life which is *free.* It is no longer the prey
of a legalistic moralism, encompassed with a host of rules
and regulations, ordered by an army of "thou shalt not's."
"Why," says Paul, "do you submit to regulations?" (Col.
2:20.) As he wrote to the Christians in Galatia: "For
freedom Christ has set us free" (Gal. 5:1). Paul would
thoroughly have agreed with Augustine's epigram: "Love
God and do what you like."

This is far from being an invitation to license, for love
is the greatest and the strongest obligation in all life.
When we know that we are loved, there are things that
we cannot do, for we could not bear to break the heart
of those who love us, or to bring tears to their eyes. We
might well defiantly face any penalty that the law might
inflict upon us for any misdeed; we would find it impossible to face the shame and the pain in the eyes of those
who love us if we made shipwreck of life.

H. G. Wells tells of the days when he was newly mar-
ried and when the sweets and the perils of success were
opening out for him. "It was as well for me," he said,
"that behind the folding doors of 12 Mornington Road
there slept one so pure and so clean that I could not bear
to stand before her squalid or drunken, unshaven, or
base." One of W. S. Gilbert's lyrics begins with the line:
"Free, yet in fetters bound." The Christian is the freest
of all men, but that love of Christ has given him the

greatest freedom of all, not the freedom to sin, but the freedom not to sin.

> Make me a captive, Lord,
> And then I shall be free.

b. It is the *cleansed* life. In it all the things that stain and soil life are put to death (Col. 3:5). Here is the difference between the Christian and the pagan view of goodness. Plato saw life as a continual tension. The soul, as he saw it, is like a charioteer, trying to drive two horses in double harness. One horse is gentle and tame and biddable; the other is wild and wayward and disobedient. And the name of the one horse is reason, and of the other, passion. Life, as he saw it, is always a struggle and a tension, in which passion is on the leash.

Any such life is always in peril, for at any moment any leash may slip or snap. The Christian view of goodness is much more radical than that. One of the labors of Hercules was to cleanse the Augean stables. In those stables for many years a vast herd of cattle had been housed, and the stables had never at any time been cleaned out. Hercules saw that for even him the task was hopeless in his own strength. There was a river nearby, and Hercules diverted the course of the river and sent its flood of purifying water surging through the stables, and so they were cleansed. The river's tide had done what man's power could not do. So the Christian does not see goodness as his own achievement; he does not see the cleansing of his life and character as his own triumph. He knows that with Christ, there enters into life a new dynamic, and that with Christ, there comes to him not only knowledge but power. Matthew Arnold could go no farther in the definition of God than to say that God is "a power not ourselves making for righteousness." That may be an inadequate description of God from the Christian point of view, but it is certainly true that, when we accept Jesus

Christ, there enters into life a power not ourselves making for righteousness, and life is cleansed and strengthened in a way that by ourselves we could never achieve.

c. It is a life in which we are *rid of the flesh,* and in which we *acquire a new nature.* The real circumcision is the putting off the body of flesh (Col. 2:11). Christians have put off the old nature and have put on the new nature (ch. 3:9–10).

The flesh is not the body, and the sins of the flesh are not what we call the fleshly, bodily, sexual sins. The body for Paul is a noble thing that can be, and is meant to be, the temple of the Holy Spirit (I Cor. 6:19). The body is capable of being made fit to be an offering and a sacrifice to God (Rom. 12:1). On the other hand, the flesh is altogether evil and can only be removed from life altogether.

It is easy to see that the flesh is not the body when we see the sins that Paul calls the sins of the flesh and the works of the flesh (Gal. 5:19). Certainly, he begins with immorality and impurity and licentiousness, but he goes on to list enmity, strife, jealousy, anger, selfishness, dissension, the party spirit. These are not sins of the flesh in the commonly accepted sense of the term.

It is a plain fact that unless there was something within us that answered to its seduction, sin would have no power over us at all. Unless there was something in us to which temptation could appeal, temptation would be quite unable to influence us and so to mislead us. This element within us to which sin appeals and which gives temptation its opportunity is what Paul calls the flesh. The flesh is that part of our nature which provides a bridgehead for the invasion of sin.

There is another way of putting this. The flesh is human nature apart from Jesus Christ; it is the Christless element and part in man. Bit by bit for the Christian, every part of human nature is brought into subjection to Jesus Christ, and when that happens, the flesh is defeated and dead. Sometimes the flesh is identified with what is called our lower human nature. But basically the flesh is that part of us, that within us, which gives sin its chance; and that part is killed and defeated when Christ takes full possession of us.

The meaning is not so very different when Paul says that we have put off the old nature and put on the new nature. To a Jew this would be a very meaningful picture. The Jews believed strongly in the doctrine of the two natures. They said that every man had two natures, two tendencies, two *yetzers,* the good nature or tendency and the bad nature or tendency. Sometimes they said that every man has two angels, a good angel who tries to draw him upward and a bad angel who seeks to drag him downward. The problem of life is not so much to control the evil nature as to eradicate it. This, says Paul, is precisely what Jesus Christ does for us. By coming to dwell within our hearts he ejects the evil nature and makes the good nature supreme; the old nature, or the old man, is banished, and the new nature, or the new man, is supreme.

Here is the answer to those who say: "It's my nature; I can't help it; I can't change myself." Harry Emerson Fosdick has a sermon entitled "No Man Need Stay the Way He Is." We are not expected to change ourselves; it is the power of Christ which alone can change us.

d. It is a life that is at one and the same time *a death and a resurrection.* Life, as Paul sees it, is a death in two senses of the term. It begins by being an *involuntary* death. We begin by being dead in trespasses (Col. 2:13). The Christian is a man who has been brought to life (Rom. 6:13). When life is dominated by sin, it is no better than a living death. But it goes on to be a *voluntary* death. The Christian is dead to sin, and alive to God in Jesus Christ (ch. 6:11). He is dead "to the elemental spirits of the universe" (Col. 2:20). He is dead and his "life is hid with Christ in God" (ch. 3:3), and because of that, all earthly sins in his life are put to death (v. 5). In Paul's language, to be dead to a thing is to cease to have any connection with it whatsoever; it is to be finally and completely done with it and to have no more contact with it; it is to be freed forever from its power. There is a whole realm of life, the whole sphere of sin, with which the Christian has no more connection than if he were a dead man.

But this voluntary death is only the negative side of the matter, and is much less than half the matter. The Christian is risen with Christ and shares Christ's new life (Col. 2:12). The Christian is alive to God in Jesus Christ. He shares the triumphant, victorious, resurrection life of his Lord.

For Paul all this was connected with the sacrament of baptism. When we think of baptism in New Testament times, certain basic facts have to be remembered.

(1) The man to be baptized was an adult, a full-grown man, with a man's mind and a man's experience.

(2) He was a man who had made a tremendous and momentous decision. He had stepped out of paganism into Christianity. He did not come, as he would nowadays, from a semi-Christian society in which Christian ideals are known and Christian ethics accepted, and in which he may even come from a Christian home. In New Testament times the man was making a clean and surgical break with his past, which might well involve the loss of his work, the enmity of his family, and the possibility of an agonizing death, and which would almost certainly involve social ostracism and persecution. In the early days no one could possibly drift into the church; to enter the church was the biggest decision a man could make.

(3) He was a man who had had a long course of instruction in the Christian faith. It is true that in The Acts baptism follows conversion with startling suddenness; but in the early church in general a man was instructed

in the facts and in the demands of the faith before he was baptized.

(4) Baptism was by total immersion. This was never insisted on as an unbreakable law. If for any reason it was impossible or inadvisable, baptism by other means was perfectly valid. The early church never made the mistake of making the efficacy of the grace of God dependent on any one way of administering a sacrament.

Now any man who came to baptism in these conditions would come with an expectant and eager heart; for him it was a thrilling moment. He descended into the water; it closed over him; it was like a symbolic burial. He emerged from the water; he saw the light again; it was like a new life. Not only that—such was his love of Jesus and such his feeling of oneness with him that in that moment he felt that he had shared the very death and resurrection of his Lord. "You were buried with him in baptism, in which you were also raised with him through faith in the working of God." (Col. 2:12.) "We were buried therefore with him by baptism into death, so that as Christ was raised from the dead by the glory of the Father, we too might walk in newness of life. . . . If we have died with Christ, we believe that we shall also live with him." (Rom. 6:4, 8.)

We cannot under modern circumstances, except in the mission field, reenact the conditions in which a man came from paganism into the church; but we can understand that experience, and we can share it. But to share it means a definite act of decision in which we identify ourselves with Jesus Christ. We may never have been dead in sin as the pagan was; nevertheless, the best of us is a sinner. And when we unite ourselves with Christ, we too die and rise again. We die to the old life and the old sins; and we rise to a new life, in which we share nothing less than the life of our risen Lord. And for those of us who practice infant baptism, that moment should be the time when we pledge ourselves in love and loyalty as members of the church of Christ.

e. It is an *upward-looking life*. Paul writes to the Colossians: "Set your minds on things that are above, not on things that are on earth" (Col. 3:2). The Greek word for "man" is *anthrōpos,* and in popular etymology the Greeks declared that *anthrōpos* literally means "the upward looker." Man's very physical form is the proof that he was designed by God to look up. Nonetheless, the fact is that there are many men who become so immersed in, and so concerned with, the things of this world that they cease to look up; their thoughts and plans and ambitions become limited to this earth.

Someone tells how a visitor to a great art gallery saw one of the cleaners at work polishing the floor. "Good morning," he said, "there are some very wonderful pictures in this gallery." "I suppose there are," the cleaner answered, "if a body had the time to look up." Surrounded by beauty, she was so busy with the floor that she never looked up. Bunyan paints the picture of the man bent double, eyes on the ground, scrabbling among the small dust of the earth, while all the time an angel stood above him offering him a golden crown—and he never saw it, because he never lifted his eyes.

The Christian is the opposite of that. The Christian's thoughts and aims and ambitions are not bounded by the horizons of this world. He sees things *sub specie aeternitatis,* "in the light of eternity." And the greatest result of that is that things at once assume their proper importances and their proper proportions. When he sees things in the light of eternity, he sees the things that really matter and the things that do not really matter. He will not be likely to spend his energy on the things that cannot satisfy, or to forget that it is possible to gain the whole world, and at the same time lose one's own soul.

f. It is a *forward-looking* life. It is a life that continually looks forward to a meeting with Jesus Christ. When Christ appears, the Christian "also will appear with him in glory" (Col. 3:4). "The day of Christ" was always something that was very much in the forefront of Paul's mind (cf. Phil. 1:10; 2:16). Paul was quite sure that life was going somewhere, and that that somewhere was the moment of confrontation with Jesus Christ.

The Epicureans believed that life was literally going nowhere except to complete extinction and annihilation; life was simply destined to go out into nothingness. The Stoics believed in an endlessly recurring cycle. At the end of every period the universe was consumed in flames, and then started all over again in exactly and precisely the same way, so that everyone—without, of course, remembering it—was destined to repeat the same life, the same actions, and the same experiences in a series of cycles forever and ever, world without end.

But Paul believed that life was going to Christ. It does not matter whether we think of this in terms of the Second Coming, or whether we think of it in terms of the time when we must rise and go and bid this earth and time farewell. In either case it is to the presence of Christ we go.

The result of this was that Paul always looked forward. "Forgetting what lies behind," he said, "and straining forward to what lies ahead, I press on toward the goal." (Phil. 3:13–14.) It is so often possible for the Christian and for the church to live a backward-looking life. Harnack once said that every great institution runs into one danger, the danger of worshiping its own past. It is so often true that Christians and churches speak and act as if all the great days lay behind. For Paul the greatest greatness lay ahead, for life was on the way to Christ.

g. It is a life whose *personal relationships are dictated by Christ*. Paul uses a vivid picture: "Let the peace of

Christ rule in your hearts" (Col. 3:15). The word he uses for "rule" is the Greek word *brabeuein*. *Brabeuein* is the word used of an umpire giving a decision. What Paul means is that, whenever there is a conflict of emotions and feelings and reactions in our hearts, the peace of Christ must be the umpire who is to say which of them is to win the day. Our relationships with other people and our attitude toward them are not to be dictated by personal reactions of vanity, the desire for prestige, the taking of offense, the feeling hurt and insulted, the desire for our place and our rights and our privileges. They are to be dictated and controlled by the peace of Christ. Our attitude toward others must be based on the decision of Christ, and the command of Christ is clear; his command is forgiving, forbearing, helping love.

h. The most impressive thing of all about this life of the Christian is the way in which *every part of it is connected with Christ*. It is lived in Christ (Col. 2:6); it is lived with Christ (v. 13). It is instructed by Christ, and the word of Christ must dwell within the Christian (ch. 3:16). When Paul is speaking of the duties of various sections of the Christian community, everything is connected with their relationship to Christ. Wives are to be subject to their husbands, "as is fitting in the Lord" (ch. 3:18). Children are to obey their parents, "for this pleases the Lord" (v. 20). Slaves are to be obedient and efficient, "fearing the Lord" (v. 22). Whatever task we have in mind, we must do it as "serving the Lord" (v. 23).

It is the Christian's relationship to Christ that dominates and dictates every other relationship in life. In his home, at his work, in his church, in his pleasure, in his friendships, in every contact with life at every point, the life of the Christian is in Christ. Christ is the atmosphere in which he lives. There could be nothing farther removed from a religion of one day, the Sunday, and of one place, the church; there is no division between the sacred and the secular; for Paul—and for us—that distinction did not, and does not, and cannot exist. "For to me to live is Christ," Paul said (Phil. 1:21), and that is what every Christian must be able to say.

i. We have kept to the end of this section what may well be Paul's most interesting statement about the life that Jesus Christ brings to a man. It is a life in which everything is said and done "in the name of the Lord Jesus." "Whatever you do, in word or deed, do everything in the name of the Lord Jesus." (Col. 3:17.) What is the meaning of this phrase "in the name of the Lord Jesus"? More than one meaning has been attached to it, and all the suggestions are interesting and challenging.

(1) Chrysostom thought that it meant "calling on the name of the Lord Jesus." If that is so, Paul will be saying: "Never do or say anything without first calling upon the help and the guidance of the Lord Jesus." This will then be advice to us to embark on no project and to engage in no task without first taking it to Jesus Christ and asking for his help and his blessing upon it. This would be far-reaching advice, for one of the great tests of any aim or desire or undertaking is, *Can* you really and honestly and without fear take it to Jesus and ask his blessing on it? If we did make a practice of taking all things to Jesus, two things would happen. First, there would be many things that we would not begin at all, for they cannot stand the test of his presence and the scrutiny of his eyes. Second, if we knew that we really could go on with the thing, we would also know that we did not go on with it alone, but in the strength of the Lord, and that which by ourselves is impossible would become possible in him.

(2) Jerome thought that it meant "in honor of the Lord Jesus." If that is so, it will mean that everything that we do ought to be designed to further the honor of Jesus Christ. We would be like truly patriotic citizens whose one desire is to enhance the good name of their country

by their life and their conduct; we would be like subjects whose only wish was to make people think more of their leader. It is indeed an acid test to ask: "Do my life and conduct bring honor or dishonor to the Lord and Master whose name I bear?"

(3) Bengel thought that it meant "in the spirit and in the character of the Lord Jesus." This is perfectly possible. In Hebrew the word "name" means very much more than the particular name by which a person happens to be called. The word "name" stands for the nature and the character of the whole person, insofar as it is known to us. That is specially true of the "name" of God. The psalmist writes, "Those who know thy name put their trust in thee" (Ps. 9:10). This, of course, cannot mean that those who know that God is called Jehovah will put their trust in him. It means that those who know the nature and the character of God as he has revealed them to men, those who know God's love and mercy and fidelity and power and holiness, will find it easy to put their whole trust in him. So this could be advice always to think and to act and to speak in the character of Jesus. Bengel goes a long way in this. He says that it means that the Christian must act in such a way that his action is the same as if Christ was doing the thing himself, or, at least, in such a way that every word and deed are offered to Christ for his approval. If that is so, this is no less than a demand that every word and action of the Christian life should reproduce the life of the Lord Jesus. The task of the Christian is to relive the life of Christ.

(4) The most interesting suggestion of all comes from a use of "in the name of" found in the papyri. A papyrus tells of the way in which the inhabitants of Assos in Troas took the oath of allegiance to the Emperor Caligula in A.D. 37. It gives the names of five elders, and then goes on to say that they took the oath for the welfare of the emperor and that they made the necessary sacrifices "in

the name of" the whole city. This can only mean "as representing" the whole city. If we take this as determining the meaning of "in the name of" in our passage, we have the great conception that in every word and deed he speaks the Christian is "the representative of Jesus Christ." This will be not very different from Paul's saying to the Corinthians that they are intended to be letters of recommendation known and read of all men (II Cor. 3:1–2). This will mean that every Christian stands for Christ, is the representative of Christ, is an advertisement for or against Christianity. By everything we say or do we either commend Christ to men or we repel men from Christ. The world looks upon us as his representatives, and that is precisely what he meant us to be.

Here is the great and awe-inspiring conception that the honor of Christ is in our hands; and our every word and action bring credit or discredit not only on ourselves but also on him. Here is the great responsibility of the Christian.

7. Paul thought of the work of Jesus Christ in terms of *revelation and of the bringing of knowledge.* To describe this, Paul uses the word *mustērion,* which is transliterated into English as the word "mystery." Christ himself is God's mystery (Col. 2:2). It is Paul's desire to declare the mystery of Christ, and for that mystery he is in prison as he writes (ch. 4:3). There is a difficulty here, because the word "mystery" is being used in a sense that is different from that which in English it ordinarily bears. In English a mystery is something that is abstruse, complicated, involved, difficult to understand. When we speak of something as mysterious we mean that it is baffling and that it defies solution and understanding and explanation. This is not the meaning of the word in Greek. The basic meaning of *mustērion* in Greek is that "which is secret." It need not be in the least difficult to understand. Given

the revelation of it, and given the key to it, it can be something of which the meaning is absolutely clear to see.

Further, in Greek the word *mustērion* developed a technical meaning. There were in the Greco-Roman world those great religious movements which were called the Mystery religions. The Mystery religions were all of the nature of Passion plays. They were all based on the story of some god or goddess who had lived and suffered and died and who had been resurrected and who had conquered death. The person who was to be initiated into a Mystery religion underwent a long period of preparation and ascetic discipline and instruction, in which the inner meaning of the story and of all its symbols was carefully explained to him. When he was brought to the highest possible peak of expectation, he was then taken to the central service of the particular Mystery religion into which he wished to be initiated. Then under conditions of cunningly organized lighting, and with a splendid liturgy, the story of the suffering, dying, rising god or goddess was played out before him. The aim was that he should become so identified with the divine figure that he too shared in those sufferings, that death, and that resurrection, that he literally became one with the divine figure, so that for him also life and death should be conquered, so that he shared in the sufferings and shared in the glory, and so entered into the very life and being of the divine. We now see quite clearly the meaning of the word "mystery" here. A mystery was something which to the outsider was meaningless and ineffective, but to the initiate was meaningful, precious, and effective to produce the greatest results. In that sense a mystery is a secret but a *revealed* secret to those to whom understanding had been granted.

Let us see, then, how this word grew in meaning, and let us try to see what Paul meant by it.

a. At its simplest a *mustērion* was simply a secret, and specially a secret that ought not to be revealed. So we read of a traitor disclosing *secrets* to the enemy (II Macc. 13:21). Disclosure of secrets is one of the wreckers of friendship (Ecclus. 22:22).

> Whoever betrays secrets destroys confidence,
>> and he will never find a congenial friend.
> Love your friend and keep faith with him;
>> but if you betray his secrets, do not run after him. . . .
> For a wound may be bandaged,
>> and there is reconciliation after abuse,
> but whoever has betrayed secrets is without hope.
>> (Ecclus. 27:16–17, 21.)

At this stage a *mustērion* is simply a secret that ought to be kept secret.

b. The second meaning of *mustērion* is a divine secret, a secret that only God can reveal. The Book of Daniel tells the story of Nebuchadnezzar's dream. He demanded that his wise men should interpret the dream, but he made his request humanly impossible by insisting that not only should they interpret the dream but also they should tell him what the dream was, without him telling them. When Daniel is brought into the matter, he and his friends pray for God's mercy concerning the mystery; the mystery is revealed to Daniel in a vision of the night; and so it is known that there is a God in heaven who reveals mysteries (Dan. 2:1–28). Here a mystery is something that no one but God can reveal.

c. So here comes the third stage in the meaning of the word. A *mustērion* is something that only God can reveal, *and that God has revealed* to those who know his mind and will. The Book of Wisdom says of wicked men:

> They did not know *the secret purposes* of God,
>> nor hope for the wages of holiness,
>> nor discern the prize for blameless souls.
>> (Wisd. of Sol. 2:22.)

It is in this last sense that Paul uses the word. When he is speaking of life after death, he says: "Lo! I tell you a mystery" (I Cor. 15:51). This is something that no man could have discovered had not God revealed it to him. The man who speaks in an unknown tongue "utters mysteries in the Spirit" (ch. 14:2). What he says is unintelligible unless God who supplied the unknown words also supplies the key. To "have prophetic powers" and to "understand all mysteries" go hand in hand (ch. 13:2). Both are the result of information given by God.

But there is one special sense in which Paul uses this word. In Ephesians he says that the mystery of God's will is his purpose to unite all things and all men in Christ (Eph. 1:9–10). The mystery of Christ is that the Gentiles are fellow heirs and members of the same body; it is the declaration of that very secret purpose of God which is the lifework of Paul (ch. 3:3–9). It is in this sense that Paul uses the word in our letter. Christ is the revealed secret of God (Col. 2:2). It is Paul's one desire that he should tell to all men the secret that Jesus Christ came to reveal, and that secret is that the love of God is universal and as wide as the world. It is his eagerness to reveal that secret that has brought Paul to the imprisonment in which he at present is (ch. 4:3).

That secret was hidden from men in previous ages (Rom. 16:25), although it was there in the prophets, although men could not see it. The supreme revelation of the purpose of God in Jesus Christ is the revelation that salvation is not a Jewish special privilege, but that it is open to all men of all races on the sole condition of faith. The secret Christ revealed, and the secret for which Paul labored and for which Paul was willing to die, is that God is not the lover of the Jews, but the lover of the souls of all men. And it is because of that revelation that we today know that we have the unhindered right of access to the love of God in Christ Jesus our Lord.

CHAPTER

8

The Church and Its Task

WE HAVE NOW to go to see how Paul conceives of the church and of the task of the church within the world.

In the writings of Paul and in the rest of the New Testament the Greek word for "church" is *ekklēsia,* and the word alone lays down the essential character of the church. The very simplest fact about the word "church" in the New Testament is the fact that it never describes a building; it is never used to mean something that is composed of stones and lime and bricks and mortar. If we had taken a New Testament Christian into a building however beautiful, and if we had said to him, "What a beautiful church!" he would not have understood what we were saying. In the New Testament the church is always people, men and women who have accepted Jesus Christ as Lord.

Further, the word *ekklēsia* is a word of two backgrounds, and from these two backgrounds there emerge certain basic truths about the church.

1. *Ekklēsia* is a word with a *Jewish* background. In the Septuagint, the Greek version of the Old Testament, the word translates a Hebrew word which in English is regularly translated as the congregation of the assembly of

101

Israel. In the Old Testament we frequently read of this assembly or congregation of Israel; and in case after case it describes the people of Israel met and assembled to hear, through Moses or one of the prophets or kings, a message from God. It is, for instance, so used for the people met to hear the commandments that Moses brought down from the mountaintop (Deut. 4:10; 9:10; 18:16; cf. I Chron. 28:8; 29:1; II Chron. 1:3; 6:3; 7:8; 20:5; 29:28). This is the characteristic word to describe Israel met as a people to receive a message and an instruction from God.

Here, then, is the first definition of the church. The worshiping church is a body of people met together to receive a message from God. There may, in fact, be many reasons why a person goes to church. Our reasons for going to church are a matter for personal self-examination. There is only one real and right reason for going to church, and that is to listen to and to receive a message from God.

2. The word *ekklēsia* has a *Greek* background, and, since the church soon became a predominantly Greek institution, this must have been a meaning that was uppermost in the minds of many of its members.

Greek government was characteristically democratic. Each city had its governing body, and frequently that body was called the *ekklēsia;* in Greece the word *ekklēsia* was not at all a sacred word; it was a word of politics and of local government. In Greek cities—for instance, in Athens—this *ekklēsia,* this governing body, consisted of all citizens of the community who had not been disfranchised. It is true that in later times a property qualification entered into the matter, but ideally all citizens were members of the *ekklēsia.* But it was impossible that all citizens should attend all meetings of the *ekklēsia.* What in practice happened was this. There were usually ten meetings a year of the *ekklēsia;* they were summoned by a trumpeter who went round the city announcing that the *ekklēsia* would meet at the usual time, on its regular date, in its own place. And the *ekklēsia* in actual fact consisted of those who accepted the invitation to be present. The church, then, consists of those who have accepted the invitation and the command of God, sent to men and offered to men in Jesus Christ.

Here, then, from the very word *ekklēsia* is a double definition of the church. The church in its worship is a body of people met and assembled to hear a message from God; the church in its composition consists of those who have accepted the invitation and command of God in Jesus Christ. But what of the function of the church in the world?

It is here that we come on what is Paul's greatest description of the church, a description that meets us in the letter to the Colossians. The church is the body of Christ (Col. 1:18, 24). Paul uses this phrase in three different ways and for three different purposes.

1. This phrase describes the church *within itself.* The church is a body. Now, a body is a complicated and complex living organism in which there are many different parts, and it can be healthy and efficient only when each part is harmoniously carrying out its own duty. The church, then, is a living organism in which there are a great many people, a great many very different people, and the church can be healthy and effective only when there is a perfect unity and harmony among all the different parts, as each carries out his own duty and his own function.

Paul was by no means the first person to discover the analogy between a body and society. Seneca (*Concerning Anger* 31) likens society to a body in which "all the members agree among each other, for it is the function of each to serve the whole." Marcus Aurelius (*Meditations* 7.13) has the same picture: "Reasonable beings, constituted for one fellowship of cooperation, are in their separated bodies analogous to the several members of the body in individual organisms." Again (*Meditations* 2.1) he says: "We have come into the world to work together like feet, like hands, like eyelids, like the rows of the upper and lower teeth."

The longest and the fullest exposition of this idea is in Livy (2.32). On an early occasion in Roman history the Roman state was split in two. The plebeians (the common people) had withdrawn from the city and had refused to take any part in its life; the whole life of the community was brought to a standstill. The senate sent Menenius Agrippa to try to persuade them to be of a better mind, and to cooperate in society. Menenius Agrippa made his appeal by means of a famous parable:

At a time when the members of the human body did not as at present unite in one plan, but each member had its own scheme and its own language, the other parts were provoked when they saw that the fruits of all their care, of all their toil and service, were applied to the use of the belly; and that the belly meanwhile remained at its ease, and did nothing but enjoy the pleasures provided for it. They therefore conspired together that the hand should not bring food to the mouth, nor the mouth receive it if offered, nor the teeth chew it. While they wished by these angry measures to subdue the body, the members themselves and the whole body were together reduced to the last stages of decay. From this it appeared that the office of the belly itself was not confined to a slothful idleness, but that it not only received nourishment but supplied it to others, conveying to every part of the body that blood on which depend our life and vigor, by distributing it equally through the veins, after having brought it to perfection by digestion of the food.

So Menenius Agrippa taught the people that society is like a body and can function only when each part of it, like the parts of the body, is acting in harmonious co-operation; and, should that cooperation turn to quarreling and competition, the welfare of the body is destroyed and death must certainly come.

It is this well-known and familiar picture that Paul takes over, and uses of the church. He works it out most fully in I Cor. 12:12–27 in the passage beginning: "Just as the body is one and has many members, and all the members of the body, though many, are one body, so it is with Christ." He has it again in Rom. 12:4–5. "For as in one body we have many members, and all the members do not have the same function, so we, though many, are one body in Christ, and individually members one of another." "We who are many are one body," he says (I Cor. 10:17). Jew and Greek have come together in one body (Eph. 2:16). "There is one body and one Spirit." (Eph. 4:4.) We are "called in the one body" (Col. 3:15).

The tremendous importance that Paul attaches to this comes out vividly in the words of the sacrament of the Lord's Supper, words that are unfortunately always misread in the liturgies. In the King James Version (the Authorized Version), on which the liturgies are founded, I Cor. 11:29 reads:

He that eateth and drinketh unworthily, eateth and drinketh damnation to himself, *not discerning the Lord's body.*

That sounds as if the particular sin in question consisted in failing to see that the bread and wine, the elements of the sacrifice, are, or represent, the body of our blessed Lord. But a reference to any of the new translations, the Revised Version, the Revised Standard Version, the New English Bible, will show that the words "the Lord's" are no true part of the text. They are absent from the great majority of the best New Testament manuscripts and appear only in the later manuscripts. The text ought to read, as in the Revised Standard Version:

Any one who eats and drinks *without discerning the body* eats and drinks judgment upon himself.

The New English Bible, however, while omitting "the Lord's," spells "Body" with a capital *B*.

In the earlier part of this chapter (I Cor. 11:17–22) Paul has just been rebuking the Corinthians because their congregation is full of sects and cliques and parties. "I hear that there are divisions among you." And here in the words of the sacrament he is reverting to that. What he is saying is: If a man takes his place at the sacrament and his share in it without discerning that the church is an undivided body, his very participation in the sacrament is a sin. If a man sits at the sacrament when there is a breach between him and a fellowman, when he is out of fellowship with his fellow Christians, when there is strife and trouble in his life and in his church, the sacrament becomes an act of blasphemy and not of grace.

Here indeed is a challenge. We cannot have communion with God unless we have communion with men. There can be no valid celebration of the Lord's Supper in any congregation that is torn by strife and faction and where there are parties and divisions. And it may be that we are compelled to say that there can be no valid celebration of the Lord's Supper so long as there are barriers that debar the members of one church from the fellowship of the Table of another. Paul gives the unity of the body of the church as high a place as that.

But let us remember in what this unity consists. It does not consist in uniformity. The point that Paul makes again and again is that in a body each member keeps and performs its own function, and in the body of the church each man keeps and performs his own function. The differences are not obliterated; they are fused and harmonized in a larger unity. Someone has put it in this way. Suppose a group of people want to sing. They can all sing different tunes and the result is discord and cacophony. They can all sing the same tune; then they can sing in unison, but unison singing is not the highest form of singing. They can form themselves into sopranos and altos and tenors and basses and then each can sing his own line and there is a glorious harmony in difference. That is a parable of the church.

The church is a body, and in a body there is unity in difference; in the churches the differences must be obliterated in a common loyalty to Christ and a common love to one another.

2. There is another set of passages in which Paul calls the church not only a body but "the body of Christ," and in them the church is described *in its relationship to the world*. "Now you are the body of Christ and individually members of it." (I Cor. 12:27.) Christ is the Head over all things for the church, "which is his body" (Eph. 1:23). All the work of the church is done, and all the officials and servants of the church are appointed, "for building up the body of Christ" (Eph. 4:12). Christ cherishes the church "because we are members of his body" (Eph. 5:30). There are two examples of this in Colossians. "He is the head of the body, the church." (Col. 1:18.) Paul's sufferings are "for the sake of his body, that is, the church" (v. 24). What is the meaning of this picture?

The body is that through which the mind works. The mind can purpose and plan, but the purposes and plans have to be translated into action, and that action is the part of the body. The body is uncontrolled and helpless without the mind, but the mind is equally helpless without the body. If, then, the church is the body of Christ, it means that the church is the body through which Christ acts within the world.

Jesus Christ is no longer here in the actual flesh, although he is powerfully present in the Spirit. That means that if Jesus Christ wishes something done, he has to find a man or an institution through whom or through which he can act. Someone must consent to be hands and feet and a mouth for Jesus Christ so that Jesus Christ can act through him. The church is quite literally the body through which Jesus Christ's work must be done.

There is a real sense in which we can speak of the helplessness of Jesus Christ. If Jesus Christ wants a child taught, or a person helped, or a message taken, he is helpless until he finds a man, a body, through which he can do the work he wishes to do. Unless he can find such a man, Jesus Christ is in the position of a head without a body, able to think, able to plan, able to yearn over men, but quite unable to do anything to turn his purposes into action.

In this sense, above all, the church is the body of Christ. It is in connection with this that Paul says two of the most startling things in the whole New Testament.

a. In Eph. 1:23 he speaks of the church "which is his body, the fulness of him who fills all in all." The word there translated "fulness" is the Greek word *plērōma*. Greek nouns that end in *-ma* are curious, because they can be either active or passive, although they are oftener passive. *Plērōma* can therefore mean either "that which is filled," or "that which fills." We could then translate this phrase, "the church that is filled by him who fills all things." But the word can be active. It is, for instance, used for the crew of a boat; and in the New Testament itself it is used of the patch that fills up the rent in the torn garment. That patch is the *plērōma* (Matt. 9:16). This phrase could then describe the church as "that which fills up him who fills all things." We believe that it is this second meaning which is the true meaning. *The church is the complement of Jesus Christ.* The church is the essential agent and instrument of Jesus Christ. It is the body without which he cannot work, and without whose cooperation his work is hindered and frustrated and even rendered impossible.

b. The second saying of Paul in this connection is even bolder and more daring. "Now I rejoice in my sufferings for your sake," he writes, "and in my flesh I complete what is lacking in Christ's afflictions, for the sake of his body, that is, the church." (Col. 1:24.) We are bound to ask, How can there be anything "lacking" in the sufferings of Christ, and how can any human being complete them and fill them up?

An analogy will make the matter clear. Suppose a doctor or a scientist or a surgeon in his laboratory or in the operating theater succeeds in discovering some drug or method or technique that will do much to lighten the toil and ease the pain of men and women in the world. That is obviously a discovery of the greatest possible benefit to mankind. But mankind can never enjoy or profit from that discovery until it is taken out into the world and made available for the people who need it. There must be men and women who are prepared, first of all, to learn all about this new discovery, and secondly, to face all the toil and the problems and even the possible sufferings of taking it out and making it available to the world; and it can often happen that devoted men and women have to undergo toil and pain and hardship and sacrifice to make the discovery known and available. There might, for instance, be a brilliant young surgeon who decided that he must take the latest surgical techniques out to the backward and distant parts of the earth, that he might there help and heal men and women who would otherwise have suffered and died; and in order to do this he will have to sacrifice what the world would call his own career, and perhaps his own health and even his own life. So it is in the case of Jesus Christ. The work of Jesus Christ is done and it requires no one to complete it; but there are millions of people who have never heard of it and who are indifferent to it. To them the good news must be taken. Every one, as Paul says, who calls on the name of the Lord will be saved. "But how are men to call upon him in whom they have not believed? And how are they to believe in him of whom they have never heard? And how are they to hear without a preacher?" (Rom. 10:14.) The work of Christ in one sense is complete, but in another sense it is not complete until all men have known of it and accepted it. He is dependent on men and women to take it out and to make it known. Sometimes, perhaps often, that task will involve some kind of sacrifice, some kind of discipline, some kind of suffering, for it is not easy to bring the message of Christ to a world that often does not want to listen to it. And he who accepts this task of bringing the message of the work of Christ to men may well be said to complete the sufferings of Christ.

If our Christian witness costs us something, that is not something to complain about. It is an honor, a privilege, and a glory, for when we suffer or sacrifice for the sake of the gospel, we are doing nothing less than sharing the sufferings of our blessed Lord.

3. It is clear that the description of the church as the body of Christ has something very important to say about *the relationship of the church to Jesus Christ.* There have always been some who took this so literally that they identified the church with the body of Christ. They insist that the church *is* the body of Christ; the church, they would say, is mystically the resurrection body of Christ. Closely allied with this line of thought is a famous phrase that says that the church is "an extension of the incarna-

tion," that just as the Son of God was incarnated in the man Jesus, so Jesus Christ is in his turn incarnated in the church.

There is a certain truth in this. But there is one fact that precludes any identification of the church with the body of Christ in any literal or mystical sense of the term. Again and again Jesus is called the head of the body. "He . . . has made him the head over all things for the church." (Eph. 1:22.) "We are to grow up in every way into him who is the head, into Christ." (Eph. 4:15.) "For the husband is the head of the wife as Christ is the head of the church." (Eph. 5:23.) This is a thought that is characteristic of the letter to the Colossians. "He is the head of the body, the church." (Col. 1:18.) The fault of the false teacher is that he does not hold "fast to the Head." Only when the Christian holds fast to the head does the church grow and develop as it ought (ch. 2:19).

This is to say that the church is under the direction of Christ, that the church serves the purposes of Christ, that the church exists to be used by Christ. This must mean that the connection of the church with Christ is so close that it could not be closer, so close that it is as close as the connection of the head with the body. But it is not identification; for the church is always serving, worshiping, praying to, kneeling before, its blessed Lord. John Foster has a story that perfectly illustrates this. An Indian came to an Indian pastor pleading to be allowed to become a member of the church. The pastor knew that this man had had no previous connection with the church, and that he had had no instruction in the faith from the church, and he therefore naturally wished to be certain that the man knew what he was doing. "Tell me," he said, "why you are so anxious to become a member of the church." The man answered: "By chance there came into my hands a copy of Luke's Gospel. I read it and I thought that I had never heard of anyone so wise and wonderful as Jesus, and I wished to take him as my Master and my Lord. But at that stage I thought that it was simply a matter between him and me and no one else. Then by chance I got a copy of the book of The Acts. Here was a difference. Luke was all about what Jesus said and did. But at the end of Luke, Jesus ascends to his Father, and The Acts begins with the same story. In The Acts, Jesus is no more on earth in the flesh. The Acts is not so much about what Jesus said and did as it is about what Peter and Paul said and did, and, above all, about what the church said and did. So," said the man, "I felt I must become a member of that church *which carries on the life of Christ.*"

Here is the great central fact. The church exists to carry on the life and work of Jesus Christ—and clearly it can never do that unless its connection with Christ is as close and living and vital and essential as the connection of the body with the head. To say that the church is the body of Christ is not to identify the church with Christ, but it is to say that the connection between the church and Christ is so organic that it is the same as the connection between the head and the body.

4. There remains one question that we must ask and answer. We have talked much about the wish of Jesus Christ to use the church for his purposes, and of the church as his instrument and agent. For what purpose does he wish to use the church? What is the place of the church in his design?

In thinking of the thought of the letter to the Ephesians, E. F. Scott discovered there two great complementary, interlocking principles. The aim of God is reconciliation, a double reconciliation, the reconciliation of men to himself and to one another. In that aim of reconciliation, God's instrument and agent is Jesus Christ. *Jesus Christ is God's instrument of reconciliation.* So Jesus Christ came to this world and lived and died and rose again for us men and for our salvation. Through his life, his sufferings, his death, and his rising again he made this reconciliation possible. But having done so, he ascended to his Father. Therefore, as we have already seen, he must have some instrument and agent through which he can work. Therefore, *Jesus Christ's instrument of reconciliation is the church.* Here are the two great interrelated principles. God's instrument of reconciliation is Christ; Christ's instrument of reconciliation is the church.

Let us see how Paul puts this. It was God's will through Jesus Christ "to reconcile to himself all things, whether on earth or in heaven" (Col. 1:20). It was God's aim "to unite all things in him [Christ], things in heaven and things on earth" (Eph. 1:10). In this world we see two situations, which are two sides of the same situation. We see a world at enmity with God, or at least completely indifferent to God; and we see a world at enmity with itself, a world in which there is tension and strife and war between class and class, and country and country, and color and color, and man and man. It is the aim of God through Christ to reconcile men to himself and to one another.

So, then, Christ makes this reconciliation possible, and the task of making it actual he gives to the church. Speaking of Jew and Gentile, Paul says of Jesus Christ: "[He] has made us both one, and has broken down the dividing wall of hostility" (Eph. 2:14). He reconciles "us both to God in one body" (v. 16). There is a perfectly definite picture here in Paul's mind. In the Temple at Jerusalem there was a series of courts leading to the Holy Place, which stood in the innermost of them. There was the Court of the Gentiles, the Court of the Women, the Court of Israel, and the Court of the Priests. Beyond the Court of the Gentiles no Gentile could go. A low dividing wall, called the *chel,* divided it from the next court; and in that wall at intervals there were set stone inscriptions forbid-

ding any Gentile to come farther, and declaring that the
penalty for so doing would be instant death. So, far from
unity, there was complete and final division. But in the
church Jew and Gentile have come together in one body.
Paul's aim is to warn "every man" and to teach "every
man" that he may present *"every man* mature in Christ"
(Col. 1:28).

Here, then, is the function of the church; it is for this
reason that the church is the body of Jesus. The church
exists that through it men may be reconciled to God in
Christ, and that in it men may be reconciled to one another
in Christ. The great double task of the church is to unite
men with God and to unite men with one another. The
church fails in its duty when it does not go *out* with the
reconciling message of Christ and when it does not gather
in all men and women of every race and class and condition in reconciliation to one another. When the church
forgets its duty of divine and human reconciliation it forgets the very reason for its existence.

9

The Life of the Christian

IN WRITING OF the newness of the Christian faith and message, Dean Inge said: "It is most significant that the gospel at once introduced a new ethical terminology. The Greek words which we translate love (or charity), joy, peace, hope, humility, are no part of the stock-in-trade of the Greek moralists before Christ. Men do not coin new words for old ideas." With the coming of Christianity a new standard of life and conduct entered into life.

Clearly, Christianity came to men with an uncompromising ethical demand. The great new privilege of being a Christian brought with it the great new responsibility of living as a Christian. It is Paul's prayer that the Colossians may have the wisdom and the understanding "to lead a life worthy of the Lord, fully pleasing to him, bearing fruit in every good work" (Col. 1:10). Christ will complete his work for his people *provided that* you continue in the faith, stable and steadfast" (v. 23). It is Paul's aim to "present every man *mature* in Christ" (v. 28). The word for "mature" is *teleios*. It has a threefold meaning. It means "full grown" as opposed to immature, a man as opposed to a mere youth. It means "fully educated" as opposed to a mere learner, one who has passed all the tests and all the examinations and is fully equipped to shoulder some task. It is used of an animal "fit to offer as a sacrifice to God." It means that which in its perfection and its completeness is a not unworthy offering to bring to God. Christianity is not an easy and a comfortable way in which the moral law has been set aside; it has an ethical demand than which none could be higher.

But further, with the need came the power; with the moral demand came the moral dynamic. Glover points out in *Christ in the Ancient World* that this is precisely what Celsus, who made a famous attack on Christianity, which Origen answered, failed to see. Celsus compared the invitation of the Mystery religions to the invitation of Christianity. The invitation of the Mystery religions was: "Whosoever has clean hands and is wise of speech," "Whosoever is pure of defilement, and whose soul is conscious of no guilt, who has lived well and righteously." The Christian invitation is: "Whosoever is a sinner, or unintelligent, or a fool—in a word, whosoever is God-forsaken, him will the Kingdom of God receive." But Celsus forgot that all that the Mystery religions could offer or demand was simply a ceremonial purity, which came from ritual washings and the like, while Christianity invited the sinner to come because it had that dynamic in it which could and did make the sinner a good man. True, Christianity invited the sinner, but it invited him not so much for what he was as for what with the help of Jesus Christ he could be.

So the Christian life was presented to men with its uncompromising moral demand and with its limitless moral dynamic.

It was a life based on the great triad—faith, love, and hope. It was based on faith in Christ Jesus, on love for men, and on hope of heaven (Col. 1:4–5). Let us look at these three great foundation stones of the Christian life.

It may be said that for Paul faith had three elements in it.

1. It consists in accepting certain facts about Jesus Christ as unalterably and unarguably true. To put it very simply, it means that we believe that Jesus Christ is the Son of God, in a quite unique relationship to God; that we therefore believe that what Jesus tells us about God is certainly true, because he knows God as no human being knows God; that through his life and death and rising again he brings men into a new relationship with God, which we call reconciliation; that every one of his demands is binding and every one of his promises is true.

2. But faith does not stop at this kind of belief which accepts as true a series of facts. It goes on completely to commit itself to these facts; it accepts them, not simply with its mind, but with its whole life. It hands life over to these facts. Let us take an analogy. I believe that the square on the hypotenuse of a right-angled triangle equals the sum of the squares on the other two sides—but that belief makes no difference to me. But I also believe that six and six make twelve and I will therefore resolutely refuse to pay one shilling and sixpence (eighteen cents) for two sixpenny bars of chocolate. This belief settles my life and my conduct. I do not simply intellectually accept it: I *act* on it. For the Christian faith is *acting* on the conviction that what Jesus Christ says and claims and offers and demands is true.

3. This faith does not come entirely from intellectual conviction, although unquestionably the mind enters into it. God gave us minds and we have to use them, as far as they will go, to think our way to certainty and to submit our beliefs to the acid test of thought. But faith for the Christian comes from *experience,* and from experience of a person. The Christian does not say, "I know *what* I have believed"; he says, "I know *whom* I have believed." Someone has used this analogy. We may ask three different people the same question: Do you believe in love? We

ask a small boy of eleven, "Do you believe in love?" "Oh, yes," he says, "my big sister's in love, and I can't get into the parlor to watch the television for her and her young man sitting there." We ask the psychologist, "Do you believe in love?" "Oh, yes," he says, "love is a condition provoked by certain mental and physical stimuli that produce certain quite identifiable reactions"—and he will go on to list and tabulate them. We go to a young man, walking home under the starlight with his girl, hand in hand, and we say to him, "Do you believe in love?" "Do I believe in love?" he answers. "Of course I do. I'm *in* love." Now these are three roads to belief. We can believe in something because we have seen it, as it were, from the outside, in someone else. We can believe in something because we can define and analyze it and take it to pieces and identify it. We can believe in something because we have experienced it, and because we know beyond all argument that it is true. Christian faith comes from the personal, living experience of a living person.

Faith, then, is the conviction, born of personal experience and encounter, that the claims, the offer, and the demands of Jesus Christ are true, and the consequent decision to commit, not simply the mind, but all of life to them.

The Christian love, like the Christian faith, is committal of the total personality to a certain attitude toward our fellowmen. The New Testament word for "love" is *agapē,* a word that scarcely exists in secular Greek at all. It is a word, as R. C. Trench has it, born in the bosom of revealed religion, a new word for a new quality. It is significant that this is not the usual Greek word for love at all; it is not any of the words that Greek uses for the love of our nearest and dearest, of our friends, or of our family. This Christian love is defined in Matt. 5:43–48. There this human love which the Christian must show is illustrated and defined by the love of God. The characteristic of the love of God which is chosen as most significant is that God makes his sun rise on the evil and the good, and sends his rain on the just and the unjust (Matt. 5:45). That is to say, there is in God an unconquerable benevolence, an undefeatable goodwill; no matter what any man is like, and no matter what any man has done, God will never seek anything but that man's good. The Christian love is that attitude to others, which, no matter whether it is refused, disregarded, rejected, insulted, injured, tortured, agonized, will never turn to hate, but will preserve only an undefeated and undefeatable goodwill.

Clearly, this is an act of the total personality. What we might call "ordinary" love is an emotional reaction; it is an experience of the heart; it is something that a man cannot help; it happens like an act of God. But this Christian love clearly demands an effort of the will and a victory over self which require the effort of the whole man, mind and heart and spirit, in order to achieve it. It is, in fact, not achievable until Jesus Christ, who is the supreme example of that unconquerable love, takes up his home and dwelling place within our hearts. The true Christian will feel no bitterness toward any man; even if a man hates him, or is indifferent to him, he cannot seek anything but the other's good.

The Christian hope is the conviction that in life there is meaning, purpose, and goal. It is the conviction that life is not a meaningless succession of random events but the progress to a goal in time and in eternity. It means that through life there runs the thread of God's purpose, and that after life there is something still to come.

There, then, are the foundations of the Christian life. Let us now look at what that life is, and what kind of people Christians must be.

There is another triad of words in Col. 1:22. The object of the life and death of Christ is to present the

Christian "holy" and "blameless" and "irreproachable" before God. Each of these words is intensely significant.

In Greek the word "holy" is *hagios;* this is also the word for "saint," which in the King James Version is the regular word for the Christian (Col. 1:2). The basic meaning of this word is "different." The Temple is "holy" because it is "different" from other buildings; the Sabbath day is "holy" because it is "different" from other days; God is supremely the "Holy One" because he is the Wholly Other, the one who in his being is different from men. So, then, first and foremost the Christian is "different."

But it is of the first importance to note wherein that difference is expressed. It is expressed, not by withdrawal from the world, but by involvement in the world. The saints, the *hagioi* (the plural form of the word), are not the saints in the desert, or in a monastery, or in a nunnery; they are the saints in "Colossae" (Col. 1:2), in "Rome" (Rom. 1:7), in "Philippi" (Phil. 1:1). The difference is to be expressed within the life of the world.

Christianity has no use for the people who are so "heavenly minded that they are of no earthly use." When John Wesley was about to retire from life to live in prayer and contemplation and meditation an older Christian said to him, "God knows nothing of solitary religion." The more Christian a man is, the more deeply involved he must be in the world. That is why the Christian must regard his day's work as every bit as important as the worship of the church. That is why the Christian must be an active member of his trade union, or his professional association. That is why the Christian must be active in politics, civic and national and international. "Everything," said Charles Péguy, "begins in mysticism and ends in politics." This is not to say that the Christian must be attached to any one party or faction. But it is to say that he is bound to express his Christianity by deeper and deeper involvement in the world.

The difference, then, is expressed in the world, but by what is the difference expressed? The saint, the *hagios,* is not only in Colossae, or Rome, or Philippi; he is also "in Christ" (Col. 1:2; cf. Phil. 1:1). There is no commoner phrase in the New Testament. What does it mean? Harnack used the analogy of the air. A man cannot live unless he is in the air and the air is in him. Just so a man cannot be a Christian unless he is in Christ and Christ is in him. We may put this very simply: for the Christian, the atmosphere of life is Christ; Christ is the very air he breathes. He will be continually conscious that he is forever in the presence of Christ. He will speak no word without remembering that Christ hears it, and do no deed without remembering that Christ sees it. He will make no decision in life without asking: "Lord, what do *you* want me to do?"

The difference of the Christian is expressed in deep involvement in life in continual awareness of the presence of his risen Lord.

The second word is the word "blameless." In Greek the word is *amōmos,* and it is a word with a very curious history. The word for "blame" in Greek is *mōmos. A* is the privative prefix, and *a-mōmos* does in Greek literally mean "without blame." But this word got itself interconnected with a Hebrew word with which it has no real connection but which has a very close relationship in sound. Every sacrifice offered to God must be "without blemish"; this phrase occurs in connection with every sacrifice (e.g., Lev. 1:3; 3:1; 4:3). Now the Hebrew word for "blemish" is *mum* (pronounced *moom*). Clearly, there is a very close affinity in sound between *mōmos* and *mum,* and so this word *amōmos* comes to mean "without blemish," and it describes a life of such radiant and lovely purity that it can be taken and offered as a gift and a sacrifice to God.

The truly Christian life is such, then, that it can be

taken and offered to God. The Christian must make his
whole life—not just his life on Sunday but his life on
every day of the week—a sacrifice and an offering to
God—and only the best is good enough to bring to
God.

The third characteristic of the Christian life is that it
is "irreproachable." The word is *anegklētos* (when g and
k come thus together they are pronounced like *ng;*
thus: *anengklētos*). The word could be translated "unimpeachable," or, as the New English Bible translates
it, "innocent."

This word has a double look in it. First, it does have
reference to men. The deacon is described by the same
Greek word in the pastoral epistles (I Tim. 3:10). The
word therefore means that the Christian must live a life
so pure and good that no one can level any charge against
him. He must be an unimpeachable advertisement for the
Christian faith. Second, the word looks beyond death, and
it means that through the work of Christ the Christian is
acquitted in the sight of God; because he has the merits
of Christ as his, he has no longer any condemnation to
dread.

So, then, the Christian life must be different; it must
be such that it can be taken and offered to God; it must
be such that it is by the power of Christ innocent before
men, and by the work of Christ innocent before God.

It remains for us to look briefly at the qualities that
should mark the Christian life. We shall look briefly at
each of them, and we shall try to define them, so that we
may try ourselves to possess them.

1. There are what we might call the personal qualities
of the Christian.

a. There is what the Revised Standard Version calls
"endurance," and what the New English Bible calls "for-
titude," and what the King James Version calls "patience"

(Col. 1:11). The variety of translations shows that it is a difficult word to translate. The word is *hupomonē*. This *hupomonē* has been defined as "a masculine constancy under trial." It is not simply the ability to bear things or even to endure them; it is not that grim and passive acceptance which can sit down, or even kneel down, and let a flood tide of misfortunes and sufferings roll over it. It is the spirit that enables a man to stand erect on his own two feet and to meet with steady eyes anything that life may bring to him, in the complete certainty that God can work all things together for good. In other words, it is the spirit that can not only accept suffering and sorrow and disappointment and even tragedy, but that can in accepting them, change them into glory. It is the spirit that is expressed in the Epilogue to Browning's *Asolando,* published on the day he died:

One who never turned his back but marched breast forward,
    Never doubted clouds would break,
Never dreamed, though right were worsted, wrong would
        triumph,
    Held we fall to rise, are baffled to fight better,
        Sleep to wake.

There are many people who can grimly endure, but *hupomonē* is the triumphant and transforming acceptance of the worst that life can do.

b. There is what the Revised Standard Version calls "patience"; the New English Bible has the same translation; the King James Version has "long-suffering" (Col. 1:11; 3:12). The word is *makrothumia*. Clearly, this word is closely kin in meaning to *hupomonē*. The distinction that the Greeks themselves made between the two words is that *hupomonē* is patience with events; *makrothumia* is patience with people. *Hupomonē* is the ability to accept any event, not simply in passive endurance, but in a way that transmutes it into glory; *makrothumia* is the ability to bear with people, not to grow angry or bitter or irritated or annoyed with them, even when they are foolish or ungrateful or even apparently hopeless.

In many ways this is the most valuable of all personal qualities. There are, no doubt, greater sins than irritability, impatience, moodiness, and short temper, but there are few sins which do greater damage to our personal relationships with other people. *Makrothumia,* patience, long-suffering, is the ability serenely to take people as they are, with all their faults and all their failings, and with all the ways in which they hurt us and wound us, and never to stop caring for them and bearing with them.

c. There is what the King James Version and the Revised Standard Version call "thanksgiving" and what the New English Bible calls "thankfulness" (Col. 2:7). The word is *eucharistia,* and we may well best see its meaning in "gratitude to God." Epictetus was a slave; he was lame, because when he was a lad his master had amused himself by twisting his leg until it broke. He was always poor and never had much of this world's wealth, but he always used to say, "What can I, a little, old, lame man, do but praise God?" God made us alive, and it is a good world to be alive in. God has brought us on our own two feet, still erect and still able to meet life, to this present hour. God has redeemed us in Jesus Christ. What greater gift than that? Let a man remind himself of God's blessings in creation, in providence, and in redemption, and he will never lack for reason to praise God.

d. Lastly of these personal qualities there is "joy" (*chara*) (Col. 1:11). The endurance and the patience of the Christian are not a grim acceptance of things. Christianity is not a cheerless acceptance of Christianity as a duty. There is radiance in the Christian life. One of her students said of Alice Freeman Palmer, the great teacher: "She made me feel as if I were bathed in sunshine." Whatever else the miracle of the changing of the water into wine at Cana of Galilee means (John 2:1–11), it certainly does mean that when Jesus Christ enters life, there comes into life, a new, sparkling vivid quality which is like changing water into wine.

There is a story of a little girl who was with her mother in a church that had a number of stained-glass windows. "Who are the people in the windows?" she whispered to her mother. "They're saints," her mother whispered back. That very same week the girl was taken by her mother to visit an old lady in the village, who was very poor, but whose life was very lovely. As they left the house, her mother said: "Well, that's a real saint you've been to see today." The girl did not say anything at the moment, but she was faced with the problem of somehow relating to each other the figures in the stained-glass windows and the little old lady in the cottage in the village. So her mind teased at it, and suddenly she saw it. "I know what a saint is," she said to her mother. "A saint is someone who lets the light shine through." That is the definition of a saint. The Christian life is not a grim acceptance of duty, as if life consisted in doing what we do not want to do, and abstaining from enjoying what we want to enjoy. The Christian life is lighted with the radiance of joy.

2. But in the Christian life there is another series of virtues, as Paul sees it, which may be said to be the qualities that govern the relationships of the Christian to other people.

a. There is what the Revised Standard Version and the New English Bible call "compassion," and what the King James Version describes by the strange phrase "bowels of mercies" (Col. 3:12). Strange as this phrase may seem, it is nonetheless very vivid. The phrase in Greek is *splagchna oiktirmou; splagchna* means the "bowels" and *oiktirmos* means "mercy" or "pity." There is a very closely kin verb, *splagchnizesthai,* which is regularly used of

Jesus, when he is said to be "moved with compassion" (Mark 1:41; 6:34; 8:2). It is the strongest word for pity in the Greek language; it quite literally means "to be moved to the depths of one's being," to be moved with a compassion that is no superficial thing but that penetrates into the innermost recesses of a man's very being, until this compassion becomes, if we might put it so, even a physical pain.

The Christian, then, is to be a man of pity, a man who cannot see suffering or need or distress without a sword of grief and pity piercing his own heart. There can be no more complete opposites than callousness and Christianity.

b. There is "kindness" (Col. 3:12). Here is the simplest of all the virtues. But when we probe a little into its meaning, there is even more in it than meets the eye. The word is *chrēstotēs*. Now, this noun is closely connected with the adjective *chrēstos*. Certainly the adjective means "kind" or "gracious." But it is significant to remember that the meaning of this adjective, especially when it is applied to things rather than to persons, is "useful." There is, then, at the back of *chrēstotēs* the idea that the Christian kindness is not simply a vague, nebulous emotion. It is a kindness that is actively useful. It is a kindness that is efficient, and an efficiency that is kind. Still another fact emerges about this word *chrēstos*. It can be used, for instance, of wine, in the sense of "mellow," without any rough harshness in it. So, then, at the back of *chrēstotēs* there is the idea that the Christian kindness has a certain mellowness in it. A person can be kind in a way that hurts and humiliates. He can be kind with what might be called a cold, impersonal, superior, institutional kindness. But the Christian kindness has in it a gracious, personal, warm effectiveness, which makes it a lovely thing both for him who gives and him who takes.

c. There is what the Revised Standard Version calls "lowliness," the King James Version "humbleness of mind," and the New English Bible "humility" (Col. 3:12). The sins of pride and of conceit are the most glaring and obvious of sins. The true Christian humility depends entirely on the applications of the right standards to life. Pride and humility depend almost entirely on the standard with which a man compares himself. If a man compares himself with his neighbor, he may emerge not ill pleased with the comparison. No doubt he is as good as his neighbor, if not a great deal better. But we must listen to the command of Jesus Christ: "You, therefore, must be perfect, as your heavenly Father is perfect" (Matt. 5:48). The Christian humility comes from the awareness that man can never be anything other than a creature in the presence of his Creator, a sinner in the presence of the holiness of God.

The Greek word for this humility is *tapeinophrosunē*, and it is a very significant fact that in Greek it does not mean "humility," but "mean-spiritedness." It has, in fact, been correctly stated that there is no word for humility in the Greek language which has not some atmosphere of that which is mean and base and low. In other words, humility was not a Greek virtue. And that was simply because the Greek did not normally possess this essentially Jewish and Christian sense of the creature in the presence of the Creator. In the *Theaetetus* (160 D), Plato quotes the saying, "Man is the measure of all things." And just because the Greek could say that, he could in effect say: "Glory to man in the highest." But in both Judaism and Christianity the virtue of humility stands in the highest place, just because for them man stands in the presence of God.

d. There is what the King James Version and the Revised Standard Version call "meekness," and what the New English Bible calls "gentleness" (Col. 3:12). The word is *prautēs* (the *a* and the *u* are pronounced separately; *pra-oo-tēs*), which is one of the most untranslatable of all Greek words.

It is not that there is not plenty of information about this word; the difficulty is to confine the meaning in any one English word. Xenophon uses it of a well-trained horse, who has learned to be obedient to the reins. Plato uses it of the sheep dog, who is gentle to his friends and to the sheep, but strong to resist enemies.

Aristotle has a great deal to say about this word. It was Aristotle's consistent habit to define all virtues as the mean between two extremes, or, as we might say, the happy medium. On the one hand, there was the extreme of excess; on the other hand, the extreme of defect; and between the mean, the virtue. So on the one hand, there is recklessness; on the other hand, there is cowardice; and the mean between them is courage. Aristotle describes this word *prautēs* as the mean in relation to anger; it describes the attitude that is neither excessive anger nor excessive angerlessness, the attitude that is always angry for the right reasons, at the right people, in the right way, and for the right length of time. In other words, this word describes the quality of the man who is always angry at the right time and never angry at the wrong time.

He is the man who has his reactions to others under perfect control. Anger is a good servant but a bad master. There is a pure anger which has been one of the world's greatest cleansing dynamics; and there is a cross, bad-tempered, uncontrolled anger which again and again has been the ruin of all personal relationships. The Christian is the man whose anger is always under control. It is only the man who can rule himself who is fit to rule or to serve others; the man who can master himself is a prince among men. The surly, irritable, bickering, uncontrolled bad temper is forbidden to the Christian; holy and selfless anger may be a Christian duty. This word *prautēs* describes the man who knows which is which, and whose temper is under the control of the Spirit of God.

e. There is *the forbearing and the forgiving spirit* (Col. 3:13). Even within a so-called Christian congregation there occur quarrels between people; even in such a place there are those who allow themselves, and even encourage themselves, to feel slighted and injured, and who are concerned with place and with prestige; even there, there are people who will not speak to one another; and even there, there are people who will say, "I will never forgive him or her for what he or she has done to me." It may be not far from the truth to say that the lesson of Christian forgiveness is the most unlearned lesson even in the Christian church. There are two reasons why the Christian must forgive.

(1) Scripture makes it quite clear that only the forgiving will be forgiven. Sometimes we ought to pause and think what we are doing when we pray the Lord's Prayer. We pray: "Forgive us our debts, as we forgive our debtors." Forgive us *as* we forgive others. That "as" means "in proportion as." Forgive me, we pray to God, in proportion as I forgive other people. This means that, if we pray this prayer while in our life there is an unhealed quarrel with some fellowman, if we pray it after we have said, "I will not forgive him for what he has done to me," if we pray it after we have said, "There are some things I can never forgive," we are deliberately praying to God *not* to forgive us. No man can pray this petition of the Lord's Prayer without the strictest self-examination, for he may well be asking God for condemnation when he prays it.

(2) Paul was quite clear why the Christians must forgive. "As the Lord has forgiven you, so you also must forgive." (Col. 3:13.) "Be kind to one another, tenderhearted, forgiving one another, as God in Christ forgave you." (Eph. 4:32.) When the Christian remembers that

for which God has forgiven him, he cannot but forgive others. Nothing anyone can do to him can equal what he in disloyalty has done to God.

Nothing brings more discredit on the church than the sight of Christians disputing with one another. Forgiveness human and divine must necessarily go hand in hand.

Finally, we must look at the rules of conduct that Paul lays down for the sphere of the family and of the day's work. The characteristic of these rules is that they lay it down that *all duty is reciprocal*. There is no such thing as a one-sided duty; or, to put it another way, there is no such thing as a privilege without a corresponding responsibility. Wives are to be subject to their husbands as a Christian duty; but equally husbands are to love their wives, and never to be harsh with them (Col. 3:18–19). Children are to obey their parents as a Christian duty; but equally fathers are not to be so critical that they simply provoke resentment and create discouragement in their children (ch. 3:20–21). Slaves are to give obedience to their masters as a Christian obligation; they are to work for no human master, but for the Lord; they are to fear no human judgment, but God's. But equally masters have to give their slaves just and fair treatment, for they must remember that they too have a Master in heaven (chs. 3:22 to 4:1).

One of the commonest and the most human of faults is that we so often demand from others standards that we are not ourselves prepared to fulfill; we are apt to be much more clearly conscious of the duty that others have to us than of the duty that we have to others; we are apt to think much more often of our rights than of our responsibilities. If we are to live the Christian life, we must live in the constant awareness that all duty is reciprocal, and we must think just as much of the duty we owe to others as of the duty they owe to us. The husband may expect respect from his wife, but she has the right to expect sympathetic love from him. The employer may expect faithful work from his employee, but the employee has the right to expect fair and human treatment from him. The parents may expect honor and obedience from their children, but the children have the right to expect understanding and encouragement from them. The life of the home and of society and of industry would become new if we set this principle ever before us as the rule of our lives.

The Message of Colossians for Today

BEFORE WE CONCLUDE our study of Colossians we must ask: What is the message of Colossians for today? What has this letter to say to us by way of advice and warning in our present situation in the middle years of the twentieth century? Is it still relevant, or has the situation changed so radically that the letter has now no more than an antiquarian interest? We believe that Colossians still has a very relevant message for today.

1. *It is a warning against all religious syncretism, and a summons to remember the absolute uniqueness of God's revelation in Jesus Christ.* We live in a time when absolute conviction is out of fashion, and when the refusal to compromise is labeled as intolerance. So the suggestion arises, Why not take the best out of every religion and out of it all make a synthesis and an amalgam that will be a universal religion? After all, it is urged, no religion can be perfect, for man always tends to make God in his own image. As long ago as the sixth century B.C., Xenophanes insisted on this very thing. The gods are the product of the imagination of man, made in man's own image. The African represents the gods as black and flat-nosed, the Thracian as blue-eyed and red-haired. "If cattle or lions had hands, so as to paint with their hands, and produce

works of art as men do, they would paint their gods, and give them bodies, in forms like their own—horses like horses, cattle like cattle." If this is so, why not take the best out of all religions and make a new universal religion of it? Syncretism is the mingling together of different religions to make one new whole.

This is a temptation that is as old as religion. It is vividly there in the Old Testament. When Israel entered the Promised Land, it was not empty. The Canaanites were there, and they had their own gods. These gods were the Baals—the word "baal" simply means "lord"— of whom the Old Testament speaks. These Baals were fertility gods; they represented the forces behind natural growth, the forces that ripened the corn and made the grape and the olive to grow, and especially the force of sex, the greatest fertility force of all.

If these gods were the fertility gods, then naturally man worshiped them by using their gifts. It became a religious act to feast and to drink and to revel. The sex act became an act of worship, and the temples were stocked with priestesses who were sacred prostitutes. They had their shrines all over the country. It was all very pleasant. Why not link Yahweh up with all this? Why not keep Yahweh, and yet accept the local worships as well? Why not amalgamate the worship of Yahweh and the worship of the Baals? After all, two gods must be better than one, and it would be as well to have the best of both worlds. The result was a creeping infection that threatened the very life of Jewish religion, and against which the prophets fought with every atom of their being. Syncretism would have destroyed Jewish religion for good and all.

The same choice came to the early Christians. In the Roman Empire the one universal worship was Caesar worship. The emperor, as it were, incarnated within himself the spirit of Rome; to worship him was to worship

Rome. So emperor worship was made universal and com-
pulsory. On a certain day every Roman citizen had to
come to a chosen place within his district and burn a
pinch of incense to the godhead of Caesar and say,
"Caesar is Lord." Rome was far from intolerant; once a
man had done that, he could have gone off and worshiped
any god he liked, so long as the worship did not conflict
with decency and good order. For the Christian the prac-
tical result of all this was that all he had to do was to say,
"Caesar is Lord," and then he could have worshiped Jesus
with no danger whatsoever. And that is precisely what the
Christians would not do. They utterly refused to make a
pleasant and safe amalgam of Christ worship and Caesar
worship, and if they had done so, Christianity would have
become simply another of the religions of which the
Empire was full.

And this is exactly the choice that came to Jesus. The
tempter showed him in his mind's eye the kingdoms of
the world. "Bow down and worship me," he said, "and I
will give you them all." It is the temptation to compromise, to accept a bargain with that which is fundamentally wrong. The answer of Jesus was that right is
right and wrong is wrong, and God alone is to be worshiped and served. (Matt. 4:8–10.)

Here is the continuous temptation, the temptation to
compromise, the temptation to make a synthesis and
amalgam of religions to please everybody, the temptation
to water down the absolutely exclusive claim of Jesus
Christ.

It is not that all other religions are things of the devil;
it may well be that they too have their partial revelation;
but when that which is perfect and complete has come,
that which is imperfect and partial must necessarily be
abandoned (I Cor. 13:10).

There comes in our day and generation the invitation
to amalgamate Christianity with, for example, spiritual-

ism or with Moral Re-Armament, to elaborate it with theosophy, to strike a bargain with Islam by agreeing that it will do to regard Jesus as a prophet. The survival of Christianity depends on the uncompromising insistence on the fact that Jesus Christ alone is the full and the unique revelation of God.

2. *It is a warning against the philosophizing of religion.* The Gnostics and the heretics wished to turn a gospel into a philosophy. Now, there is this one basic difference between a religion and a philosophy. The search of a philosophy is for abstract truth; the search of religion is for a person.

It is perfectly true that religion must stand the test of the mind. I once heard a famous theologian deliver a public lecture, presumably of the greatest profundity, certainly of the deepest obscurity. I asked him afterward, "Do you really expect ordinary people to have any idea of what you are talking about?" "Oh, no," he said. "Is, then," I asked, "religion something that only the select few can understand?" "Oh, no," he said, "you must not confuse *religion* with the *conceptualization of religion.*" This is to say that you can separate religion from the philosophic presuppositions and implications and explanations that lie beneath religion. There is *religion* and there is a *philosophy of religion.* This is no doubt true, but the danger enters in when the statement of the philosophy becomes more important than the experience of the religion. We are seldom quite free from the danger of forgetting that Jesus said, "Follow me," not, "Discuss me." In a discussion-group age we are at least sometimes in danger of substituting intellectual interest for religious experience.

3. *It is a warning against all religious snobbery.* We have seen that the Colossian heretics worked on the assumption that religion is bound to be for the select few, whereas Paul was obsessed with the allness of Christianity.

In the modern church there can be a twofold snobbery. There can be what we might call an *ecclesiastical* snobbery. There are certain congregations that will often actually say that a certain type of hymn and a certain type of preaching and a certain type of service is all right for the people in a mission hall, but it is not what they are used to and it will not do for them. There are certain congregations that, to put it frankly, are terrified of the word "evangelical," and afraid of all *emotion*. They believe themselves to be above and beyond "that kind of thing." There can be what we might call a social *snobbery*. There is in the church today a confusion between religion and respectability; there are tragically few churches in which there is anything like a cross section of the population; religion tends to be stratified, just as society is stratified. Stephen Neill writes in his Lenten book, *The Eternal Dimension,* of the ambition of a typical American student: "To get a good job as soon as I leave college, and to marry a nice girl straightaway, and to live in a nice house, in a nice locality (we don't talk about suburbs anymore) among nice people all of about the same age and in the same income bracket, and to have some nice children, and to join a couple of nice clubs, and to join a nice church which will make no demands on me whatever beyond general conformity and a reasonable level of financial support; and so everything will be just fine." It is not altogether unfair, nor is it a total caricature. There are those for whom the church is little more than the hallmark of respectability. The great danger of the modern church is that it is a one-class church—middle class—with the top and the bottom ends of the social scale lost. The church is on the way out unless it discovers again Paul's allness of the gospel.

4. *It is a continual warning that religion and action go hand in hand, or, to put it in slightly more technical lan-*

guage, that theology and ethics cannot be separated. It is
a very significant fact that all Paul's letters culminate in
an ethical chapter packed with ethical demands. Even so
theological a letter as Romans culminates in the ethics of
Rom., ch. 12. It may well be that we have understated
the sheer ethical effort of Christianity. It is the very same
Paul who so stresses justification by faith who insists on
the ethical demand of Christianity. It is certainly true
that no man is saved *by* works, but it is equally certainly
true that every man ought to be saved *for* works, and that
if his alleged salvation does not issue in an ethical life, it
is no true salvation.

There is a certain type of evangelism that has much to
answer for. Its invitation is: "Come to Jesus Christ, and
you will find rest and peace and joy." That is a dangerous
half-truth. It is certainly true that through Jesus Christ
we learn that God is not our enemy but our friend, and
the fear of God is banished by the love of God. But it is
also true that, when a man accepts Jesus Christ, then the
struggle begins. As Browning has it:

> When the fight begins within himself,
> A man's worth something.

With the coming of Christ into life there enters a new
demand, a new challenge, a new standard, a new responsibility that was not there before.

The fundamental meaning of justification by faith is
that a man is brought into a right relationship with God
not by any efforts of his own but simply and solely by the
love of God. But the plain fact of life is that there is
nothing in this world that lays such an obligation upon a
man as love does. The man who is loved is forever and
forever under obligation to try to deserve that love. The
man whom God loves is under obligation to live the life
that God would wish his loved one to live. A man does

not know what love is unless he yearns to bring joy to his lover.

5. *Lastly, it teaches us that we cannot separate the church and the marketplace.* The insistence of Colossians is that the Christian must be a Christian in the world quite as much as in the church. This is something that even yet so many fail to see. Religion, worship, God, are things confined and even imprisoned within the church. Max Warren in *The Christian Imperative* tells how an African headmaster wrote to thank a friend of his for a course of talks he had given in an African school. "We greatly appreciate your helpful talks," he wrote, "on the application of the teaching of Jesus in our agricultural work and hygiene, as well as in spiritual things. Until now we regarded agriculture and hygiene as secular subjects, without any connection with Christianity." The real, acid question is not, What does Christianity make a man within the church? but, What does Christianity make a man in the office, the shop, the factory, the shipyard, the school, the golf course, the dance hall, the home? It is life that Jesus promises, and life cannot be confined to any part of life; life permeates all life. The challenge to the Christian is to make all life one continuous act of worship to God.

Like the rest of the Bible, Colossians has a message that cannot go out of date.

Appendix

A Note on the Genuineness of Colossians

I T IS USUAL to discuss the genuineness and the authenticity of a book in the introduction to it and at the beginning. But in the case of Colossians most of the arguments that are used in the attempt to disprove its Pauline authorship come from its contents, and therefore cannot be properly weighed and evaluated until its contents are known. It has therefore seemed better to leave the discussion of this question until the end. Four main arguments have been used against the genuineness of Colossians.

1. It is argued that its *vocabulary* is not Pauline. In Colossians there are 33 words that occur nowhere else in the New Testament at all, 17 of them in the second chapter alone; and there are more than 50 words that do not occur elsewhere in Paul's letters. The answer to this argument is twofold.

First, this is, in fact, almost exactly the same proportion of new words as occurs in the letters of Paul about which there is no dispute, for example, in Galatians and Corinthians. The proportion of new words may seem high, but it is not abnormal.

Second, even if the proportion were high, it has to be remembered that in the discussion of new subjects Paul needed new words. A man's vocabulary is bound to be expanding. If he writes to new people about new things, he will obviously require new words. Any new elements in the vocabulary of Colossians are amply explained by the new things Paul had to say.

2. It is argued that the *style* is not Pauline. It is true that the style is not the same as that of Romans, Galatians, and Corinthians. It is more difficult and involved; it is grander and more rhetorical; it is more diffuse; and it is definitely harder to translate. But again there are certain things to be said.

In Colossians, Paul was writing to people whom he had never seen or met. He would naturally write more carefully than he would to old friends. The subject matter, the all-sufficiency of Jesus Christ, is exalted, and would naturally have an effect on his style. And perhaps the most important point of all to bear in mind is that Paul wrote this letter in prison. It was not dashed off in the haste of his missionary journeys. It was written when he had all the time in the world to write it, or to dictate it. One would expect on perfectly general grounds that the style would be more elaborate than the style of letters written at white heat in the middle of a journey.

In any event, style is always a dangerous criterion. Are we to argue that because Shakespeare wrote *The Midsummer Night's Dream* he could not have written *Lear* or *Hamlet*? A man is not an automaton geared to write only in one way; his style will alter with circumstances. And in the circumstances of its writing and in the nature of its contents there is nothing in Colossians that would preclude the belief that Paul wrote it.

3. It is argued that the *thought* is not Pauline. It is argued that the Christology of Colossians is far too advanced, and that it is beyond anything else that Paul ever produced. It is argued that the idea of the Christ of crea-

tion is much more connected with the Logos doctrine of the Fourth Gospel, which did not emerge until around A.D. 100.

This argument is only valid on the assumption that the thought of Paul was static and incapable of new development to meet new situations. Paul believed in the unsearchable riches of Christ. The plain fact is that the situation that met Paul in Colossae was a situation that had not met him anywhere before. That situation compelled him to think out his own belief about Jesus in order to meet it. It is always true that a man only grasps and possesses as much of the truth as circumstances compel him to lay hold of. The Colossian heretics' attack on the all-sufficiency of Jesus Christ was precisely that which was needed to stimulate Paul to think out his answer. And in any event, all that is in Colossians in fuller form exists in embryo and in germ in I Cor 8:6: "For us there is one God, the Father, from whom are all things and for whom we exist, and one Lord, Jesus Christ, through whom are all things and through whom we exist." That is exactly the summary and undeveloped statement of what Paul is saying in Colossians.

The thought of Colossians is no barrier to its Pauline authorship unless we insist that Paul's thought was quite static and incapable of any development, and surely that is an assumption that it is impossible to make.

4. It is argued that the particular *heresy* involved in Colossians did not emerge until much later in the history of the church. It is true that the great Gnostic systems are later in their emergence; but it is equally true that the differentiation between spirit and matter, the essential dualism, which is the essence of the Colossian heresy, had a long, long history, and was in existence centuries before Christianity entered the world. It is not any definite system which Paul is attacking; it is a tendency of thought,

and that tendency had a long history before it began to affect Christian doctrine.

The fact is that there is nothing in Colossians which makes the Pauline authorship of it impossible, or even unlikely. We may have no hesitation in accepting it as a letter written by Paul.